LIFE BY THE LYNN

By
Christie Loney

"The Caretakers Cabin"
Sketch by John Hoyt

xulon
PRESS

DEDICATION

This wee book is dedicated with very much love to three people who have a most special place in my heart, Thomas and Mary Fitterer and Vickie Kerr.

I first met you Thomas, when you were the Principal at the Auke Bay Elementary School and I was chairperson of the P.T.A. Who would have dreamed that one day many years later, you would be my boss at the Shrine of St Therese. You are a man of great faith, much discernment and wisdom that often guided my footsteps through rough terrain to find sure footing.

Mary, you have always been there for me, albeit in the background, providing a listening ear, loving encouragement and hugs. I have lost count of how many times Bob and I have sat at your table comparing notes as we shared the journey of faith with you and Thomas over a cup of tea or a delicious meal.

Vickie, there would be no story to write, had you not been a woman of much faith, discernment and persistence. You were so sure we were to be the Caretakers at the Shrine of St Therese that you would not give up and prayed it into being. Thank you for your constant love and friendship down through the years and across the miles.

We have all dreamed many dreams together and I recall that when I shared another "episode" in the adventure of living Thomas would say, "Another chapter for that book you will one day write."

So here it is, and this is not even the half of it – to tell it all would fill many books, as the dreams, the planning, and the adventures of faith continue on.

Both Bob and I look forward to that day we will sit with you at the table of our Lord and Savior, Jesus Christ, and see all the dreams and plans fulfilled according to His perfect plan, but until then, may the Lord bless all of you for being such a blessing to us.

In His love,
Christie Loney

CONTENTS

ACKNOWLEDGEMENTS

I n many ways this book has been a family affair.
The cover design was created by our son, David. This is
my second book, and he did such a beautiful job with the
cover of my first one, I asked if he would bless me with
another. John Hoyt gave us permission to use a sketch he did
of the Caretakers Cabin, when he and his wife, Luci Shaw
visited us. David incorporated this sketch into his design for
the front cover of the book. David, you did it again; it is
beautiful, thanks so very much.

Daughter, Sharon Fish, and granddaughter, Hannah Fish
provided *invaluable* hours of help with page formatting,
proof reading, and editing. When I tried to say thank you
Hannah said, "I love doing it." Even so, their work of love
is greatly appreciated. Also, Thomas Fitterer has carefully
read every page for accuracy of dates, and facts, and has
provided much needed historical information. Thank you so
very much. If there are any mistakes, they are entirely mine.

Granddaughter, Bethany Fish, helped me choose the pictures to insert. It was fun, but challenging, to go through
eight years worth of photos knowing we could only choose
ten or less for the book. Bethany has a photographer's eye
for what is *best!* Thank you.

Granddaughter Scarlett has been sketching since she was
a toddler, and I knew when I began this book she would be

the perfect person to ask to illustrate one of the stories. I was right; it is absolutely perfect. Thank you Scarlett for your time and patience. I hope you enjoy seeing your work in print. I do. ☺

There are twenty prayer warriors who have prayed this book into being. While most of them are not blood relatives, they are very much "family" to me. Every day for the past year or more, they have been faithfully providing me with encouragement and support. Very special thanks to Rick and Delores Anderson, Bjorn and Liz Christie-Johnston, Sharon Fish, Thomas and Mary Fitterer, Libby Hanaford, Dorothy Hendrix, Jeff and Kristin Hock, Tom and Melody Kirchner, Andrew and Marilyn Loney, Julie Orsi, Dan and Kathie Sellars, and Ken and Marion Shay.

Last, but most definitely not least, my most faithful prayer warrior, provider of my breakfast every morning with a smile, the one who is my biggest fan, yet also able to give honest critique; is Bob, my husband of fifty years. I love you.

But, perhaps my husband is not last on the list. The first and last, the one without whom there would have been no call, and no story to tell, is my Lord and Saviour, Jesus Christ. He is the one who has been my constant companion from beginning to end. He provides the inspiration for every-thing I write, and to Him be the glory today, and forever and always. Amen!

INTRODUCTION

While this is a book about life as Caretakers at the Shrine of St Therese, it is also about how the Lord touches lives through the beauty of His creation. It is a book about people who enjoy the outdoors and majesty of snowcapped mountains while having a picnic at the beach, watching salmon spawning, diving to the depths of the ocean floor or just sitting watching the waves wash over the rocks. It is about people discovering a place of peace and tranquility that draws the soul to seek for deeper meaning in life.

As you laugh at the antics of the animals, enjoy the variety of visitors, walk a trail of tears with the hurt and wounded, and find that real men love to vacuum, I pray you will also discover that place of peace and deeper meaning in your own life that leads to "the obedience that comes from faith." May grace and peace be like bookends around your days as we enjoy this journey together.

As previously mentioned, I have had twenty precious people who committed a prayer covering for the writing of this book. My commitment to them was to send out a monthly update and list of prayer needs. In my first e-mail to them a scripture popped into my head:

Romans 1:5-7. "Through Him and for His name's sake, we received grace and apostleship to call people from among the Gentiles to the obedience that comes from faith. And you also are among those who are called to belong to Jesus Christ...Grace and peace to you from God our Father and the Lord Jesus Christ."

Those words have become a thread woven throughout the pages of this book and a prayer for each of you, the readers. As you read maybe you will discover something of the mystery and glory of God from our "Life by the Lynn."

LIFE BY THE LYNN

PART ONE

A HISTORY LESSON

T here is a small booklet entitled *"Shrine of St Therese –
The History of a Dream"* that was published in 1989 by
the Shrine of St. Therese. The following facts and excerpts
are shared from this book with the permission of Thomas
Fitterer, retired Director of the Shrine of St. Therese.

"The dream, the plan, and the construction of the Shrine
of St. Therese, is the story of people working together. It
is a pioneer story typical of our country. Likewise, it is the
continuation of the Christian story of people 'in search for
meaning.'"

It is a place "Well known to local residents as a place of
special beauty. Looking over Lynn Canal, it is a place to take
friends and relatives when they visit. But more than that, it
is a place listed on tourist brochures and draws people from
all over the world. It is also well known as a place for those
"hoping to catch the silvers and salmon off the rocks of the
island, divers wanting to find crabs, and picnickers in search
of sunshine. Many go there to let the majesty of God and the
nature He created wash over them like a healing balm."

Over 50 years ago Bishop Crimont approved the process
of naming the site a Shrine to St. Therese of Lisieux. 'Many
favors and blessings, even miracles over the years, have
been attributed to her intercession.' She was known as "The
Little Flower of Jesus" and died in 1897. Bishop Crimont

was from St Therese's native land, France and knew some of her family.

But there was a man with a dream long before all this happened.

Father William G. LeVasseur (a cabin at the Shrine is named after him) envisioned a place where people could come and retreat from the business of the world; a place that would 'Call people to a greater devotion to God.'

There was no such place in Alaska at this time. So five acres of forested land were secured from the government twenty-three miles out the Glacier Highway from Juneau and work began in August, 1932. In 1935 five more acres, adjacent to the original tract, were obtained.

I was struck with the fact that, "The original cost estimate for the retreat house and chapel was only $3,000 not including furnishings." Wow! But remember this was during the depression years, so an appeal for funding was undertaken. "A.B. Cain of Juneau, editor of *The Alaska Catholic*", sent out as many as 500 letters each week. Father LeVasseur wrote personal replies to each of the donors." It is interesting to note that many of the requests for donations for this project were sent from a post office established on the Shrine premises. This postal service was provided for people living in this isolated area from 1938-1946, Father Le Vasseur was the official postmaster.

The building is still standing today and is used as a place for small groups or individual retreatants. It is still called "The Post Office."

One man worthy of note in the history of the Shrine is Father Hubbard, who was known as the "Glacier Priest" "In correspondence dated 3rd October, 1940, Father LeVasseur tells of how Father Hubbard visited for 10 days and gave a lecture that raised $200 for the Shrine. The letter tells of Father Hubbard's promise to help and refers to a generator he was sending."

As noted in the beginning, this is a story of people working together.

"The donation of 35,000 feet of lumber from a Juneau firm provided materials for several small cabins that could be used for private retreats and extra accommodations."

According to a letter sent to His Holiness Pope Pius X11 in September, 1939 "A volunteer from New York City, George Murphy, cleared off all the trees and stumps, dug the foundation and helped pour the concrete in preparation for the stone structure which was to be built the following year. All this labour was done entirely free of charge, and without any previous experience in this line of work. Murphy returned in 1938 and assisted in building the Chapel."

The Chapel was to be built on what was then called Crow Island, now named Shrine Island, which was 400 feet from the mainland. So before the work on the Chapel could even begin a causeway had to be constructed, this did not begin until the summer of 1935. "It proved to be quite an engineering feat owing to the high tides and severe storms." A man named D.P. "Doc" Holden was foreman of the Chapel project. He had this to say, "We had a hundred dollar truck, wheelbarrow, a mortar box, mortar hoe, rope and falls for hoisting stone and a handmade skip. There were some bad times, but the work continued, and in time the chapel structure was completed."

The *Alaska Daily Press* of 28th October, 1941 tells of the first Mass in the Shrine chapel. Father LeVasseur said the Mass and Bishop Crimont blessed the bronze statue that was donated by the Nick Bez family in memory of their daughter.

"Bishop Crimont, who died in 1945 after more than 50 years missionary work in Alaska, is buried in the crypt under the main altar."

The Shrine has had its ups and downs. "By 1962, the priests' retreats were no longer held at the Shrine. The buildings deteriorated and the Diocese did not have money to maintain the facility. A major renovation took place in 1968 and 1969...the summers of 1972 and 1973 saw the Shrine staffed and planned programs offered to the community. Once again, the financial drain of the Shrine maintenance forced its closure in the spring of 1985." However, "A small group of people uneasy about abandoning the vision of the Shrine would not let the dream die. They met on 24th July, 1985 with the goal of once again making the Shrine a viable retreat center." With careful thought, prayer and preparation, this small group wrote the following statement of purpose for the Shrine of St. Therese:

"Located in an area of exceptional beauty and solitude, the Shrine will be a place of spiritual refuge and retreat for the diocese of Juneau, other religious groups and when possible for other groups utilizing it with reverence and care."

This is where *my story* begins!

A CALL

In the spring of 1988 my husband had recently lost his job and we were wondering, "What now?"

"I know this job is for you," my longtime friend Vickie seemed almost desperate for me to understand. "I had a dream and the Lord spoke to me about you having this job."

"But the retreat centre is Catholic and we are Presbyterians," I reminded her.

"I know that, but the Lord has shown me that you and Bob are the couple for the job, so *please call Thomas.*" It seemed urgent, so reluctantly I rang his number.

"We are not really looking for any more applicants, in fact we have almost made our choice, but I will send you the forms and you can fill them out and send them in," he cheerfully replied. I gave him our address and hung up. The forms duly arrived, but the deadline date for application had passed. They had enough names anyway so why bother; besides I did not have time. Our daughter was getting married, our youngest was leaving for college, the family dog of fifteen years had just died…my plate was full. I threw the forms in the trash!

The summer passed. The wedding was over. Our son had left for college and once again there was time to pause and think. What now? The phone rang, "Christie, did you ring Thomas, I know this job is for you and Bob?"

"But Vicki they hired a young couple back in April, the position is filled."

"Yes, yes, I know," she said, "but they have resigned, this job is yours, please ring Thomas." "Nothing ventured, nothing gained," we thought, but it all seemed so unlikely. Thomas reminded me he had sent me an application, but never got it back. "I trashed it," I confessed. A second form arrived in the mail, we filled it out and with hearts daring to hope mailed it off to Thomas and the Shrine committee.

It had been years since we had been to the Shrine of St. Therese retreat centre, and it was a sunny day, so spur of the moment we packed a picnic lunch and drove the eight miles out the road, down the tree lined driveway to the awesome beach-side beauty below. The Caretakers log cabin lured us to the door. A timid knock brought a young woman in response, "Can I help you?" she enquired. Feeling suddenly rather foolish, we explained that we had applied for the Caretakers position, and wondered if we might see the house. We learned that she and her husband were the couple who had just recently resigned, and she seemed excited and eager to show us around. She was very gracious, and answered our many questions. An hour or so later she hugged us goodbye, and with an encouraging smile said, "I really hope you get the job." Now our hearts were more than hopeful. We dared to believe.

At the interview a few days later, it seemed our being Presbyterians was an asset, for Bishop Michael Kenny shared with us his vision of a more ecumenical outreach for the Shrine of St.Therese.

The rest is history. Vicki was right, it *was* our job! God had filled the position until our hectic summer schedule was over. His timing is always perfect; in September 1988 we accepted the call to be Presbyterian Caretakers at a Catholic Retreat Centre.

Awesome God!

A MISSION MOVE

Tuesday, 4th October, 1988 our predecessors, Larry and Ginny moved out of the Caretakers Cabin, and we began painting and preparing on Wednesday the 5th for the big *mission move!*

We had lived in our home at Mile15.8 Glacier Highway since summer 1970. It was home! For eighteen years life had happened in this house on the hill above Auke Bay Recreation Area, a place we claimed as "Our Beach." The blind corner, on this stretch of the highway, was lovingly called "Loney's Corner" by our friends. It was where our four children had grown up, and from here they headed off to college. Now three of the four were already married, and our grandson was already two years old.

When Bob and I got married in 1961, we agreed that we wanted to have children and after they were grown and out of the nest we wanted to be missionaries. But our idea of missions was going overseas, yet here we were, moving eight miles out the road.

However it clearly was a *mission move*, a call to ministry as Caretakers at a Retreat Centre. Little did we know how much our lives would change as we began this new adventure of faith!

Saturday 8th October was set as our "big move" day. Bud Morris, Jim Sepel, Rev. Leon and David Thompson, Ed Van

Patten, and Roger Fitzjarrald from Chapel – by – the - Lake Presbyterian Church arrived early to help us make the move, while Marilyn Kiefer and Ellen Jones provided delicious meals to keep us going. Already the "ecumenical outreach" that Bishop Michael Kenny envisioned had begun.

The first retreat group arrived on 13th October. But before that day dawned we had many training sessions, learning how to use the huge stove, walking through the facilities, discovering where everything was kept and *exactly* what it meant to be a "Caretaker". Around the edges of our care-taking days we continued unpacking a lifetime of what had represented "home" since 1970.

On unpacking dishes, pots and pans etc I discovered I had to change my plans mid-stream when I realized that the cupboard space in our log cabin home at the Shrine of St Therese was not configured the same as our 15.8 Glacier Highway kitchen.

Now what?

"I have *always* had these dishes together in the cup-board," I thought to myself. "These spices *have never been separated before*, how will I find things if I don't *keep them together in the same place they have always lived?"* What a dilemma! This was just the first of *many hurdles* as we began the "Mission Move."

Up to now there had been little time to really consider the *daily reality* of the move. Now it was in my face as I sat on the floor trying to put things in space that didn't work. But I learned that the Lord has an amazing way of helping us leap such hurdles with practical solutions. After all He is the Master Planner.

If you have never been at this place before and are per-haps making a move, consider leaving behind all your pre-conceived notions of keeping life in your box labeled "never change." It doesn't work! As I let go of my kitchen of the past and *really* saw the kitchen I was now in, and allowed myself to enjoy the challenge of change, it became fun.

Pat Spence, a longtime friend, came and helped me do some wallpapering. Others helped with painting bathrooms. I made curtains for the bedrooms, hung pictures and plates on the walls and watched the log cabin take on a *"Better Homes and Gardens"* kind of look. Within days it had the feel of home when we walked in the door.

However, we still had a huge learning curve. We began to settle into a new life while still keeping those important connections with our community and church family. One of those connections was working at a Christian school part time. Along with being a pre-school teacher's assistant, I was responsible for the Latch Key program in the mornings, which meant being at the school at 7am so parents could drop off their kids on their way to work. Each day breakfast was provided and a safe place for the children prior to beginning their school day. Our "Mission Move" meant eight more miles added on to my already very early morning drive to the Mendenhall valley school. Monday-Friday I worked 7-1 pm at the school, then a fourteen mile drive out the highway to the Shrine of St. Therese, down the tree lined driveway to put on my Caretaker *Missionary* Hat.

I quickly discovered I was working *seven days a week!*

In the past being a teacher meant having weekends off, however as a Caretaker this was often the busiest time of the week as many groups enjoyed retreats at the Shrine.

Shopping, cooking, cleaning, painting, plumbing, gardening, vacuuming, stripping beds, and re-making beds... **This is a *mission* move?** It was a question we asked more than once in those first days as we settled into our new environment and pondered the role of being a missionary caretaker.

WHO'S WHO

THE BISHOP

Who was Bishop Michael Kenny?

Thomas Fitterer has begun compiling some information which he has graciously shared with me, so this, along with our own experiences of Bishop Michael, provides a little background on a man who was dearly loved by so many, not only in the Juneau Diocese, but in many other parts of the world.

He was born 26ᵗʰ June, 1937, in Hollywood, California to parents Arthur and Esther Kenny. "His schooling included attending St. Joseph's College in Menlo Park. He had been ordained to the priesthood in 1963 in Santa Rosa by Bishop Leo Maher. There he became involved with the different parishes, as well as teaching high school." Perhaps this fact helps explain his great love for high school students and one that lasted his entire life. Let me digress for a moment and share what Ken Koelsch, a teacher and director of the Juneau Douglas High School musicals, had to say about the Bishop's relationship with students.

"Bishop Kenny always adjusted his busy schedule to attend one of the opening weekend performances of the spring musical. He came backstage and congratulated the cast and always took time to follow up his compliments with a letter to the cast and to the newspaper. Every year he sat down front in the first row. One had to be careful, however, where you discussed the upcoming musicals with him. Last year, both of us were in a large jury selection room in the Court building when I told him we were going to do '*Guys and Dolls*'. To the amazement of the 49 other potential jurors, he sang the entire repertoire of '*Guys and Dolls*', beginning with '*We Got the Horse Right Here*' to '*Sit Down, You're Rocking the Boat*.' This year I bumped into the Bishop on the street, suffering my normal memory lapse I told him we were doing '*Camelot*.' He launched into '*C'est Moi*' and ended with arms outstretched singing '*Camelot*'. Farewell friend, we will not forget."

In 1991 the front row seat and the spring musical, "Anything Goes" was dedicated to Bishop Michael Kenny by the cast and crew.

Now back to his earlier life - "Recognizing his many gifts and skills, particularly people skills, Kenny was named chancellor of the Santa Rosa Diocese in 1972, and was made a monsignor in 1977. Michael Kenny had been the first priest ordained in the new Santa Rosa Diocese, and his Santa Rosa friends and parishioners were especially pleased that he attained the role of bishop."

"To add to the celebration, Kenny, along with twenty-five other men, was selected to receive his Episcopal consecration in Rome by Pope John Paul 11 on 27th May, 1979 this special day was attended by many from the Diocese of Santa Rosa and the Diocese of Juneau. He was officially installed as Bishop in Juneau on 15th June, 1979."

Bishop Michael was known for his "joyful and positive display of heartfelt love, an out-flowing sense of compassion, an unbounded energy, a delight in good humor, and a dashing display of wit that could more than hold its own." Add to this enviable list of gifts, his amazing ability to serve up a gourmet meal with seeming ease. Each year at the annual auction to raise funds for the Shrine, an item that caught everyone's attention, and kept the bidding lively, was one of these gourmet meals at the Bishop's home.

In an article Bishop Michael wrote in November, 1994 for *"The Inside Passage"*, the Diocese of Juneau newspaper, we glean a glimpse into this man's heart and character development. "I remember a sun filled California day a very long time ago. I was not yet three years old. A poor old man came to our back door looking for something to eat. I can still see him. Heavy, drab colored clothes piled on his back, a soiled hat, dirty hands and face. My mother smiled and asked him to wait outside while she put together a lunch. She made a sandwich of considerable proportions. "Would you like to bring it to the man? Delighted to be involved, I carried the sandwich to the door. As I reached up to hand it to the fellow it slipped out of my hand and slopped down on the cement landing, all of its contents spilling out on the ground. Then it happened. Without making a sound, the man looked down at the ruined sandwich and began to cry. I am sure my mother must have made him another sandwich. I don't recall. But for years after, I included a child's 'God bless the poor old man' in my bedtime prayers."

"When I was 4 ½ years old, the Japanese bombed Pearl Harbor. From everyone's reaction I sensed something terrible was unfolding. Some weeks later, I found the cleaning lady, who came once a week to help my mother, crying as she dusted the shelves by our living room fireplace. I went and told my mother. She said she knew, but that I would not understand and that there was nothing we could do. But I still remember. And now I know the reason for the woman's tears. She was a Japanese-American. That day was the last time I saw her."

Bishop Kenny goes on to share some other vignettes of tears and how they touched his life, tears of joy at the gift of a fur coat for his mother, tears of gratitude for all the help of friends and neighbors during his mother's serious illness "Little children cry a great deal," he said, "I am sure I am no exception. But the tears I remember best were not my own."

Bishop Michael's mother died when he was only seven years old, this experience, at such a young age, perhaps continued shaping a heart already full of compassion and concern for others.

"As Bishop of 6,000 Southeast Alaskan Catholics, and as one who reached across denominational lines as well as community, state, national and international contacts and needs, Kenny bridged his relationships in many and varied ways. He assumed different rolls depending on the circumstances. It might be as priest and bishop, pastoral counselor, preacher, peacemaker, social justice provider, participant and promoter of the arts, friend…"

"He believed that God was one who put out the invitation for all to come to a deeper level of love and appreciation of life…Michael Kenny stated that 'God will never, never force His way into our lives and He seeks our love which is never love if it is not freely given…Think: the poor will not be cared for if we do not look after them. The sick will not be healed if we do not act as instruments of mercy. There will be no justice if we do not act justly. There will be no peace if we are not peacemakers.'"

Bishop Michael Kenny was known as one who served in all the above roles. He was particularly well known for speaking his mind in regard to the futility of war. "He was asked and willingly said yes to traveling to Iraq to help in the intervention of the release of foreign hostages in the Middle East.

In 1991 he was involved, before Operation Desert Storm commenced, in helping to try and bring about peace in Iraq…Kenny expressed concern that this war could bring a 'warring element' amongst the local people of Juneau and encouraged them to 'not make enemies of one another.'"

In many ways, because he was outspoken, he was seen as a Bishop who lived outside the box of what is considered the norm for a man in his position. In fact, I believe this is what made him unique and so very approachable by people from every walk of life. In relationship to native people in Alaska he said, "I humbly ask for forgiveness for the blunders and the times Catholic missionaries may have failed to appreciate the depth of Native spirituality or affirm the value of Native language, culture, art, dance and music. I personally ask forgiveness for those occasions when I have been insensitive to the needs of our Native peoples or failed to see and treat them as equals."

My intent here is not to give all the details of the life and work of this man of God, but I hope when Thomas completes his booklet on the life of Bishop Crimont and Bishop Kenny you will avail yourselves of it and learn more about their amazing lives.

However, before we leave and move on to other "Who's Who" on my list, this background would be sadly lacking if I did not share something about Bishop Kenny's strong faith which was the rock on which he stood and from which he gained strength to be the man of God that indeed he was.

"In reflecting on his past life, Michael Kenny related how he went to Mass daily from 4th grade on and engaged in substantial prayer and spiritual reading at this early age. 'I firmly believe the Lord enters into lives and calls you to something for the sake of others. I have a very intimate and very strong relationship with Jesus Christ.' *"Juneau Empire"* 22nd October, 1981. "Having that intimate relationship with his Lord, Michael Kenny, priest and bishop and lover of humanity, was especially appreciative of the Shrine of St. Therese as Holy Ground, a place of 'refuge and retreat.' He felt a close connection with Bishop Crimont, for Joseph Crimont also had a faith-filled relationship with Jesus and chose to be interred beneath the Shrine altar following his death."

"Not knowing the condition of the crypt where Bishop Crimont was interred, Bishop Kenny gave permission for the 300 pound concrete crypt entrance lid to be removed in January, 1995 to investigate the crypt's interior."

Just today as I sat having lunch with my husband, Bob, and I was telling him I was writing about Bishop Michael, he said, "Did you write about his premonition of his death?" When I said I did not know about any premonition he told me this story.

"While we were working on the crypt, Bishop Michael had just come out from a time of prayer inside the crypt and said to me, 'Make sure name plates are put on the tombs, mine and Bishop Crimont's.' I told him, "Don't you think that Bishop Hurley will be here first, besides you are very healthy?' Bishop Kenny replied, 'Well I don't think Bishop Hurley will want to be buried here and besides I might die first of an aneurysm."

Later, at a Shrine Board meeting he also spoke to Thomas Fitterer about the name plates, "Consideration should be given to putting name plates on the ends of the tombs the next time someone is interred in the crypt – and it will probably be me – but I am not in any hurry," he said. That board meeting was held on 7th February, 1995.

On Sunday, 19th February, Bishop Kenny was in Jordan. "Bishop Kenny had celebrated his 'Last Supper' as he presided at a Mass just four hours prior to his death. While visiting the Roman ruins of Jerash later that day, Bishop Kenny suddenly became nauseous, lost color, collapsed and died. Just a day before his death, Michael Kenny had visited Mount Nebo to view the site of the Promised Land found in the scriptures (Tradition has it that Moses, too, had climbed this Mount to look over the Promised Land before he died)".

His body was entombed 4th March, 1995 in the Shrine crypt, at the exact same location that he had knelt in prayer just five weeks prior and where he had predicted the possibility he might die of an aneurysm. The report of death said he died of an aneurysm!

In my memory box of our years at the Shrine I have a precious card dated February, 1995. It was sent to me, following a gathering at the Shrine Lodge for a time of reflection after Bishop Michael died.

"Dear Christie,

I treasured our evening at the Shrine. We walked out to the Chapel at 10pm and the little island was surrounded by starlight and dancing northern lights – a beautiful vessel, I thought, to hold the memories and the body of Bishop Kenny. I also treasured your reflection. We laughed a lot that night as we told stories about his antics and sense of humor but your reflection told why we loved him so much. He had such a depth of caring and was deeply connected to our God, and he very actively - and always personally - showed us God. It was a rare moment you shared with him, wrapped in solitude, filled with wonder. Thank you for sharing that moment with us. I've kept a copy for myself and to share with others if I may?

I wish you peace, Margie Beadle.

Below is the sharing to which Margie refers:

Bishop Michael Kenny

"Bishop Michael was a man always on the go, hard to catch up with, or so it seemed to me, until last year at the priest's retreat here at the Shrine of St. Therese.

It was early in the morning, and I was sitting by the window having my quiet time. The sun was just beginning to touch the snow-capped peaks across the water, when I noticed a solitary figure walking along the grassy edge of the beach in front of our log cabin. Ever so slowly, step by step, and back and forth he walked. His eyes never lifted to the majestic mountains or the beauty around him. He seemed deep in thought, eyes glued to the open pages of a book he held. There was a marked steadiness to his pace, almost as though with each step he took, the words he read were being imprinted on his mind and in his heart.

I watched for over half an hour, deeply touched, and knew a sense of communion of my own as the Bishop walked with God. There was no sense of intrusion, but rather an awesome wonder that the Holy was present to both of us.

Bishop Michael was a man who walked with God and where God is its Holy. *He was a holy man and this is Holy ground.* I praise God for the gift and privilege of knowing him. He blessed my life and I will miss him"

Christie Loney.

A Psalm of Life"

Lives of great men all remind us

We can make our lives sublime

And departing, leave behind us

Footprints on the sands of time,

Footprints, that perhaps another,

Sailing o'er life's solemn main,

A forlorn and shipwrecked brother,

Seeing, shall take heart again.

-H.W Longfellow

THE DIRECTOR:

The following information is taken from notes sent to me by Thomas when I requested some background prior to his becoming the Director for the Shrine of St Therese. I am truly amazed as I look back over some of what I wrote through the years as Caretaker Reports how the Lord was at work in and through this ministry and mission with Thomas as the Director.

As previously mentioned, it is my hope and prayer that as you read this book you will learn something of the mystery and glory of God being revealed through the pages of history and the people who crossed our paths. Thomas and his wife Mary were two of those who crossed our path in a most significant way. Reading through Thomas's notes it became quite clear that it is the work of the Holy Spirit in our lives that makes this mystery known.

"You asked me to write about my journey in becoming the Director of the Shrine of St Therese and some highlights of those years. I believe I would best need to provide some lead up information to help with understanding of what took place prior to the Shrine Directors position.

In the mid 1970's I was led to partake in a Life in the Spirit session at St Paul's Catholic Church, (incidentally Bob and I also attended these events) I remember being 'prayed over' and one of the members of the team said, 'Relax and receive the gift of the Holy Spirit.' Following that experience, as I spent daily time with scripture and prayer and continued to partake in prayer group meetings, my faith and fervor grew."

Thomas shared that one scripture in particular spoke to him at this time.

Luke 4: 18-19 "The Spirit of the Lord has been given to me, for He has anointed me, He has sent me to bring the good news to the poor, to proclaim liberty to the captives, and to the blind new sight, to set the downtrodden free, to proclaim the Lord's year of favor."

In many ways it was in Thomas's daily expression of this scripture that we found our lives intersecting at a deeper level. We first met Thomas when he was the Principal of Auke Bay Elementary school. "Having taught in the public schools for several years," Thomas shares, "I sensed that I was to consider returning to a college environment to receive either a Masters in Counseling or in some form of Christian counseling. To do this I would need to receive a leave of absence from the Juneau School District."

As a result of much prayer and discernment leave was granted, and he and Mary left Juneau for Spokane, Washington. He has this to say of that period in his life, "Prior to leaving Juneau friends had given us a plaque with the statement; *'God will not lead you where the grace of God will not sustain you.'* This really was a statement of truth which we needed to refer back to many times during our sojourn to Spokane and Gonzaga. When we found a place to live in Spokane, we posted this plaque in full view of our kitchen table and referred to it often during our time there."

So they left Juneau in August 1982, three kids, Mary, Thomas and a dog named Rat. But like many plans we make, they "aft gaen aglae" Robert Burns. In other words, they don't go exactly according to our expectations. So it was "one year ended and another started and our courses of study were not yet complete for graduation purposes.

This change required that the Juneau School District be notified that I would be resigning from the District." It also necessitated another step of faith in the Fitterer journey as they would no longer have income or benefits being pro- vided by the District.

"As we moved into the last half of the second year, we began to check out job openings that would coincide with my Masters in the Spirituality field. Oftentimes, the good

Lord speaks to one in particular or unique ways so that a person can hear. In hind sight, I realized that there was a message coming to me during this time that I was not fully understanding. God was trying to guide me through a poignant dream."

Suffice it to say that this dream did indeed come to pass. In May, 1984 Thomas attended a Jesuit Retreat in Spokane and it was during this time he was given a sense of direction as doors closed to one place and opened to return to Juneau. So in August, 1984 they found themselves back in their own home in Lemon Creek, Juneau, Alaska.

"Having returned and become somewhat resettled, I converted part of one side of the garage into a waiting room and office area, for I felt a call to offer individuals a holistic Christian prayer focused counseling/spiritual direction ministry..." The months sailed by after our return from Spokane and during prayer one day there was an inner spiritual awareness that the Shrine of St Therese was to be reactivated in some way spiritually. Mary, while we were still in Spokane heard that the Shrine was hard pressed financially and perhaps going up for sale for it was draining the Diocese of Juneau considerably, said that she thought the Shrine could be a full time retreat center. It did not speak to me at the time other than to remember her sharing this. But now in prayer, the prompting was coming my way and I sensed that I was to pursue a plan to help bring new life to the Shrine."

Thomas goes on to tell of a Knights of Columbus gathering at the Shrine in either fall 1984 or spring 1985, he does not recall exact dates, but he and a man named Tom Satre began discussing spiritual needs and possibilities for reactivating the Shrine. "Tom (Satre) had experienced the Shrine of St Therese as a young person and deeply remembered how blessed he and other Satre family members were to have the Shrine in their midst."

The outcome of this conversation had a far-reaching affect.

"With what seemed to be a spiritual push for reactivating the Shrine, Tom Satre, Fr.Bill Finn, Tony Thomas and I met 24th July, 1985 at our home 5933 Lund Street. During our meeting, with much fervor from all four members present, we decided to approach Bishop Michael Kenny with the proposition of reactivating the Shrine as a full time retreat center. Satre prepared minutes of our meeting and sent them to Bishop Kenny and requested an appointment to meet with him. Bishop Kenny gladly welcomed Tom and gave his blessings to the cause. He personally desired to partake in the Shrine Committee that would formulate a plan for reactivation of the Shrine and recommended we not delay with planning for this to be done. This was good news for sure, with joy in our hearts little time was wasted before the next meeting was scheduled...Two additional persons who truly loved the Shrine, and were long term supporters of this place, Katherine Shaw and Florence Mynarski, were invited to participate on the Shrine Committee. They met with Bishop Michael Kenny and Thomas Fitterer August 15th at the Bishop's house. There were so many immediate needs to be addressed for the re-opening of this sacred space for retreats and renewal, it required the committee to pray and plan for each task that needed to be addressed and to prioritize what was most important.

Some of the beginning topics addressed at that meeting pertained to seeking Shrine caretakers, setting up a simple financial plan, some physical and environmental needs, and requirements for a Shrine director, to list a few. The request for persons to apply for the caretaking position was announced in the Diocese Catholic church bulletins and the Diocese newspaper, *"The Inside Passage."*

Three couples applied and Gene and Terri Sweigarts were accepted and moved into the Caretakers house on site in October, 1985. This was a season of much adjustment on the part of all involved. Thomas relates that the Shrine committee inherited a financial account that was in the red, so one very large undertaking was to come up with ways to generate funds as well as restore the Shrine facilities into a working and welcoming retreat center. "Sensing the magnitude of the task of making needed improvements at the Shrine, the Committee decided to hold two meetings per month to handle business. It was important to address the physical needs of the Shrine; even more important, was the need to focus on the spiritual plans for utilizing this Holy ground. At the December, 1985 Shrine Committee meeting, Bishop Kenny moved that 'Thomas Fitterer be appointed the Interim Manager of the Shrine of St Therese facility for the first six month period of 1986 and the Shrine Committee would give full consideration in the search of a Shrine Director in the meantime.'"

The outcome of this proposal was a letter, from Thomas and Mary, to the Board suggesting they serve as a couple. So it was that on January 15th 1986 the Shrine Board approved Thomas and Mary Fitterer as Interim Managers for six months. One of their first roles was to get word out about the plan for opening the Shrine facilities on 15th March, 1986, and formulate the Mission Statement.

What started out as an "interim" position, became a full time job for Thomas from 1985-2009. When asked to comment on some highlights of these years he said, "So many good things took place, not because of me, but because God provided...If a plan is in line with God's will, doors will open and close appropriately if we do not get in the way but assist in the 'little way' as *St Therese of Lisieux* would say." "I believe one of the most wonderful things about the Shrine was the fact that so many people participated in little and big ways to give life to this special place. Donations of time, skills and funds have been outstanding over the years...

I know the good Lord used the place to draw forth good from all these people, and as they 'gave' in so many ways – they grew more blessed and the Shrine grew more blessed. The Shrine of St Therese, built on a foundation of love truly reveals the fruits of love…when love is given it increases and continues to multiply and to bless others." Thomas says, "I believe the Holy Spirit welcomes all and is present to all in unique ways as they visit the Shrine. I have always taken great joy in the fact that this Holy Ground can address the wandering person who drives out the road and stops in for a visit and is touched by the Lord, the fisherperson, the beach comber, or on sunny days, the beach recliner those on retreat at one of the facilities…the child who tosses rocks in to the sea or digs in the sand…this place reaches the 'inner hearts' of people…even the hardness of an inner heart is often softened by a visit to the Shrine…it speaks of the glory and the goodness, the love and the mercy of God."

In June, 2009 Thomas retired as Director. The mystery and glory of God comes through as a blessing to all who have shared the journey with Thomas and Mary Fitterer.

THE SHRINE COMMITTEE

In writing about Thomas Fitterer, the now retired director of the Shrine of St Therese, I learned quite a bit about the history of the Shrine Committee.

In May, 1994, at the recommendation of Sister Judy Gomila it became known as The Shrine of St Therese Board, its members were constituted as The Board of Directors.

But what I want to share about this august group of men and women is not the details of their evolving but rather our experience of them on a daily basis in our role as Caretakers at the Shrine over a period of 8 ½ years.

The following people were very active members during our years as Caretakers. Some were still active when we resigned in 1997 and others resigned along the way.

Bill Brown, Bonnie Elder, Sr.Judy Gomila, Bishop Michael Kenny, John Monagle, Florence Mynarski, Tom Satre, and of course our boss Thomas Fitterer made up the Board when we began. There were other special folk who were added during our tenure. Judy Whittaker, Tisket Sesslar, Gordon Preecs, Rose Marie Good, Kathy Hedges, Ronald Skillings, Vince Hansen, Lisle Hebert, Marijo Toner, Fr. Michael Nash (he assumed Bishop Michael Kenny's position on the Board when the Bishop died), Janis Burns Buyarski and Joe Kyle.

As I write their names many memories flash on the screen of my mind. For example, I will never sing "I've got a River of Life" without thinking of Sr. Judy who had a most unique way of making it come alive with actions that still make me smile. Or Florence Mynarski's wit and wisdom that kept meetings moving along and her heart desire for keeping the Juneau Borough roads clear of litter. Many days we would see her walking along with a plastic bag picking up debris, rain or shine it mattered not; she was a woman who put her hands to the task whatever it might be.

I remember Marijo Toner for her faithfulness as a worker on the annual Shrine Clean up Day. Cleaning cupboards and windows and just enjoying the fellowship. She always had a smile. John Monagle is best remembered for his smiles, hugs and amazing sense of humor. He always had a tale to tell and has an amazing memory. You can't help loving this man. He too was a worker.

Rose Marie Good and Kathy Hedges along with Janis Burns Buyarski were great supporters and I appreciated them for the many weeds they pulled, flowers they planted and the encouraging words they often spoke when we crossed paths. Tisket Sesslar and her late husband, Chuck, were among the faithful prayer warriors we could always rely on, and I enjoyed using the gift of note cards with her art work on display that found their way onto my desk.

The men on the board were available at the drop of a hat if we had a need, especially Tom Satre. We would never have survived the winter months without his snow plowing. He would just drive down the road, get the job done and be gone before we could get out the door and thank him. Tom was not one to blow his own horn, but he was always there, steady and dependable.

The names and faces of each one of you, whether I have singled you out for mention or not, is indelibly engraved on our hearts. There are many untold tales of God's love and grace that will be told in heaven of each one of these precious saints.

THE CARETAKERS

Once again, I am indebted to Thomas Fitterer for help with background and information on the Caretakers at the Shrine of St Therese. Thank you Thomas!

According to Thomas, there is not much reliable information available regarding names and dates of Caretakers prior to 1970 or 1971 when Jerry and Sharon Jones took up residence in the Caretakers cabin. They served in this role for 13 years ending their term in 1983 or 1984. While the Shrine was perhaps not a fully functioning retreat center during some of those years the Jones family provided a very important presence on site.

As we have already learned in the previous pages, in 1984 a sense of revival began at the Shrine and following a short vacancy after the Jones family resigned, Gene and Teri Sweigert brought new life to the facilities when they began their Caretaking duties in September, 1985. They served and cared for all who came on retreat until January, 1988 when once again there was a brief vacancy and the Board advertized for new Caretakers. Larry and Ginny Sackett answered the call and were duly installed in May, 1988. A few months later they bought a house in Auke Bay and resigned as caretakers. However Ginny continued to be involved with the Shrine serving as a member on the Board from September, 1989 until March, 1990.

So once again there was a vacancy, and in a tale already told, we applied and were accepted as the new Caretakers in October, 1988. We thought we would live and die on the job, but the Lord had other plans and in June, 1996 we moved out of the Caretakers Cabin and overseas to China. Within days of our departure Chuck and Joan Gasparak took on the role. We enjoyed a few days prior to leaving helping them get acquainted and left knowing the place was in excellent hands. They jumped in feet first and Joan was well known for her wonderful cookies. Unfortunately Joan became sick and died in November, 1998. She was greatly missed not only by her family, but also by the Shrine community. Chuck's daughter, Julie, moved in with him and helped out following her mother's death. They continued to provide loving care for all who came on retreat until June, 2000.

Following in their footsteps were Jody and Marcia Liliedalh, who faithfully served as Caretakers until August, 2005 when Steve and Janet Olmstead came to fill the vacancy. We knew Steve and Janet quite well as he was pastor at Chapel by the Lake when we lived in Juneau and attended that church. They too felt called to other pastures and resigned in May, 2007. Once again the position was advertized and Jack and Jeanne Jordan came on board in December, 2007 and as of this writing January, 2011 they still enjoy the role of Caretakers at the Shrine of St Therese.

Also worthy of note are ones who from time to time filled the role of caretaking, Jim Rebar, Sam Bertoni, an almost fulltime volunteer, and many others, enabling Caretakers a time out, opportunity for vacation, or much needed help during times of sickness and ill health. Thomas Fitterer not only filled the Directors shoes but *often* stepped in to assist when extra hands were needed to keep the facilities clean and meals on the table for back to back groups with little time in-between.

But, as with the list of Board members, these are just dates and names, what does a Caretaker really do? Prior to leaving the Shrine in 1996 I prepared a "Manual for Caretakers" with "Helps and Hints on how to be a Care-giving Caretaker." It included the Shrine Statement of Purpose, the Caretakers Contract, a Job Description, also some Policies and Practices and What to do When Problems Arise etc.

At the close of this manual in Section 16 "Last but not Least" I wrote;

Three Things to Remember

1. You are not alone.

   God is with you. He is in control (Proverbs 3:5) then I gave some examples of how we had seen God change the schedule and provide for needs throughout our years as Caretakers.

2. We are a *Team*.

   Thomas and others are just a phone call away.

3. The Little Way.

   The things that count, a word of encouragement, a note of thanks, flowers on the table, a cup of tea, a helping hand, a word of prayer, or just being there in a time of need, this is what matters. Give a smile, it costs nothing, but gives much, it enriches those who receive without making poorer those who give.

While I am sure this manual is now quite outdated, as many things have changed over the years since we left, I believe these last three things are still worthy of note in the on-going ministry and mission as Caretakers.

However, we are still left with the question, "What does a caretaker do?"

Keep reading. Part Two of this wee book will provide a glimpse into *Life by the Lynn* where we were most privileged to be called, *"The Caretakers."*

AN INSTALLATION

Before we move into Part Two of this book and the answer to "What does a Caretaker do?" I would like to share with you a most inspiring and significant day in our *Life by the Lynn*. While our work as Caretakers at the Shrine of St Therese began in October, 1988 it was not until 25th June, 1989 that we were officially installed. The following letter was sent to Chapel by the Lake members from Thomas Fitterer.

Installation of Caretakers – House Blessing

"Dear Chapel-by-the-Lake Members,

It is with considerable pleasure that the Shrine of St Therese Committee invites members of your congregation to gather with your pastor, Reverend Leon Thompson, Bishop Michael Kenny, and members of the Roman Catholic Community, along with others of different denominations, to officially install Bob and Christie Loney as Shrine Caretakers. This installation service will take place in the Chapel on Shrine Island. Following the ceremony, persons will be invited to attend a Blessing of the Caretakers' House and an informal finger-food dessert which you are asked to bring for the occasion.

The installation service will begin at 7:30pm. Do allow time to safely travel from your house to the Shrine and kindly join us for this special event.

The Caretaker Installation service is a first for the Shrine of St Therese; the coming together of different Christians is not a first, but such occasions are truly blessed events. Sincerely, Thomas P. Fitterer."

Prior to the event Bob and I met with Bishop Michael Kenny and Thomas to plan the service and were most appreciative to be allowed to choose scripture readings, hymns and praise songs that had special meaning for us.

It was an amazing time of inter-denominational fellowship led by Bishop Michael Kenny and our pastor, Rev. Leon Thompson. We processed into the Chapel and down the aisle to the singing of "How Great Thou Art" followed by more singing of praise music led by the music groups from both St Paul's and the Chapel by the Lake.

Bishop Kenny gave a warm welcome, followed by an opening prayer by Rev. Thompson. Then I read Isaiah 40:28-31 and 41:8-10 and the congregation participated in a Responsive Reading of Psalm 8.

A highlight of the evening for us was a beautiful duet sung by our daughter and son-in-love, Sharon and Bob Fish. My husband, Bob, read the 2nd Scripture, Romans 12:1-13 and Rev. Leon Thompson read the Gospel message. This was followed by a Homily given by Bishop Michael Kenny related to the role of being a servant for the Lord. The actual "Rite of Commissioning the Caretakers at the Shrine of St Therese" was as follows:

Opening Prayer:

Reader: God of all good things you have given this Diocese a very great gift, the Shrine of St Therese, a spiritual refuge of exceptional beauty and solitude. Like its name sake, Therese of Lisieux, the Shrine too, has been an inspiration to many ordinary people. We praise and thank you for this constant reminder that nothing can separate us from you, O God.

Tonight we gather in your Name for we share the responsibility of ministering to others through the Shrine. Two among us have responded in a special way to your call to service. Through involvement as caretakers for this cherished land, its rustic buildings and loving people, Bob and Christie Loney are ambassadors for the spread of your Good News. We now call them forth to give them a commission to this ministry.

Prayer of the Community:

Leader: As a sign of our concern and support, let us join in a few moments of quiet prayer for these members of our staff and for all who generously give of themselves on behalf of the Shrine of St Therese. Pause.

Commitment of the Loneys'

Leader: You have been called to become ministers among our people. Will you promise to grow as disciples by making every effort to tend to your own spiritual needs?

Loneys: I will.

Leader: Will you fulfill all the responsibilities of your ministry as outlined in your job descriptions and work in collaboration with the Director and the Shrine Committee?

Loneys: I will.

Leader: Will you pledge your support to uphold the purposes and values for which the Shrine stands and to promote a Christian atmosphere?

Loneys: I will.

Leader: Then on behalf of our Diocese and in the name of the Shrine Committee, we accept your commitment to participate in the ministry of the Shrine of St Therese.

Bishop Michael Kenny and Rev Leon Thompson each anointed one of us with oil as they spoke these words over us: "Receive this as a sign of your commitment. It carries our promise of support through witness, work and prayer. Continue to let the light of Christ shine through you."

Philippians 1:3-6
Hymn 310 "Take My Life and Let it be consecrated"

Final Prayer and Blessing
Closing Hymn #269 "Jesus Calls Us"

The evening celebration after the House Blessing was held in the main Lodge and ended up being more of a pot-luck dinner instead of just finger-foods as originally planned. The place was packed and we felt incredibly blessed by all who gathered for this momentous occasion in our lives.

LIFE BY THE LYNN

PART TWO

A Place of Quiet Rest

THERE IS A PLACE OF QUIET REST

P art two of this book is about the actual day-to-day life of Caretakers at the Shrine of St Therese and what they do; but perhaps before I begin to tell some Caretaking tales you might like to know a bit about the buildings where we spent many hours with mops and buckets, hammer and nails, and other tools of the trade. In fact my hubby reminded me, one of the fun parts of our installation was when Bishop Kenny and our pastor, Leon Thompson, each dedicated and handed us "tools" as symbols of the tasks to which we were being called – a broom and a shovel. You will read more about the shovel later!

While the title of this chapter may be somewhat deceptive regarding our role, none-the-less, it is the peace and quiet of the Shrine of St Therese that lures people to life by the Lynn, and the buildings themselves are part of the charm and character of this restorative retreat spot representing a little piece of heaven on earth.

When we moved to the Shrine there were quite a number of buildings in various stages of repair and disrepair. There were basically six buildings, including the Caretakers Cabin, that were in regular use: The Lodge, Post Office Cabin, Le Vasseur Cabin, The Hermitage, and the Shrine Island Chapel.

There were also three outhouses, two of which were used mostly by tourists and visitors but also those who rented the Le Vasseur as it had no indoor plumbing or electricity. The third outhouse was across the river to the south of the Caretakers cabin. Today there is a wonderful new facility for the public behind the Caretakers cabin – Restrooms with flushing toilets and sinks.

Scattered around the grounds were a number of other very small log structures as well as a very large storage/ garage building behind and to the south of the Caretakers cabin. One of these small log buildings which was only about 6x7' held a great deal of fascination for me and over the weeks and months a dream emerged regarding this wee cabin, which I will share later on.

The main building where people could stay was, and still is, The Lodge. Research reveals that; "Previous to the 1932 ground-breaking for this lodge, there was no building in Alaska suitable for the religious laity to gather for spiritual retreats. With the initial securing of 5 acres from the government, and eventually with an act of the U.S. Congress allowing the catholic Bishop to purchase a total of 46.5 acres (at $2.50 per acre) that need began to be filled. Henry Myers and Peter Ludwig were contracted to cut the logs and build this "Retreat House," and by 1935 most of the work was completed."

But it would be quite some time before there was central heat and running water. This amazing building has seen some changes over time but the basic log structure remains the same. It can sleep 22 people in 10 bedrooms 8 of which are upstairs and reached by a beautiful rustic wooden spiral staircase. Today each of the bedrooms has its own washbasin and there are also two shower rooms with basin and toilet facilities at each end of the building upstairs and one downstairs that is handicap accessible. In fact many of the buildings are now handicap accessible as are all the trails around the retreat grounds.

All the rooms have windows from which to enjoy God's glorious creation. The beachside rooms have an unsurpassed view of ocean and snow-capped mountains beyond while those on the hill side enjoy the verdant green forest grandeur.

There is a huge rock fireplace at one end of the main meeting room and the other end provides space for meals to be served at round tables. Off the main room is a large kitchen with which we became very familiar as many groups requested that meals be provided. Off the kitchen is a large pantry room and on through this you come to a room for storing a variety of items needed for repairs and maintenance of the facilities.

The Post Office cabin, as previously stated, was actually a functioning post office as the result of a number of people petitioning the U.S. Government. Father LeVasseur, S.J. who was a local priest, became the first postmaster. It no longer functions as a Post Office today, however the sign hanging above the front door "Post Office" was quite often the source of visitors asking us if they could mail a letter or postcard.

The Post Office can sleep 6 and has 2 bedrooms, one being a bed/living/dining room. It has a nice wee kitchen with a 4 burner gas stove and oven, small refrigerator, toaster, and all the necessary cooking items and dishes for 6 people. There is also a small bathroom with sink, toilet and shower facilities off the second bedroom. There are times when the main lodge is not large enough for groups and this cabin provides a wonderful place for over flow. It is also a wonderful spot for a honeymoon.

By decision of the current Shrine Board, The Post Office was totally gutted this past winter, 2010, and when it is renovated it will be quite changed, (at least inside) from what it was when we were Caretaker's. However I understand they have not changed the name; it is still The Post Office.

The LeVasseur Cabin, named for Father William G. LeVasseur, has seen a variety of uses. It also was used for a short period as a Post Office as well as a retreat master's residence. When we first took on the role of Caretakers this building was in much need of repairs, and one of Bob's first tasks was wiring this cabin for electricity. For most of our years at the Shrine it was used for day and overnight retreats, usually singles or a couple of people. During the summer months it was used for fellowship and refreshments following the Liturgy in the Shrine Chapel. Now it is the Shrine Gift Shop.

The Hermitage yet another small 13'x17' cabin, is used mostly by singles or a couple. It too was in need of repair and Bob spent quite a bit of time wiring it for electricity and doing other repairs. Before the bridge was built across the stream to the south of the Caretakers cabin, renters of The Hermitage needed wellingtons to ford the stream. This was really a "rough it" type of retreat in those days, with water provided in gallon jugs and a torch to see the way to the nearby outhouse. However even with electricity it is still a very rustic cabin. It is heated with a wood burning stove. There is no cooking stove or refrigerator. There is a picnic table outside the front door and a beach fire-pit for outdoor cooking. Renters now use public restrooms with flushing toilets and sinks 180' away. But like all the Shrine facilities it has a glorious view of the Lynn Canal and is secluded among the trees for a wonderful place of quiet and refuge from the noise of the world.

Since we left the Shrine another smaller Lodge/Cabin was built in 2000 for large groups called The Jubilee Cabin. It was the first new facility constructed since the initial building phase of the 1930's. It can accommodate 13 people in comfortable beds but 20 could be managed with the use of a sofa bed and some twin mattresses. It has a very modern kitchen, dining and meeting area with doors out to a deck area. This beautiful log cabin is situated on a high spot with a glorious view overlooking the Lynn Canal. The first floor is ADA (handicap) compliant. While we are unfamiliar with this cabin from a Caretakers vantage point, I have enjoyed participating in or leading several retreats in the Jubilee Cabin.

One other building, new since we lived at the Shrine, is the Little Flower Retreat Cabin. This is a very deluxe cottage hidden off the main paths along a road on the southern boundary of the Shrine grounds. It has a spectacular view of the Inside Passage waters. This building, which is seventy feet above the shoreline, is very secluded and private. It was primarily funded by donations from Vivian Kirkevold in memory of her daughter Heidi. "Her intent was to provide funds to build a special place for people, particularly couples to come for holistic renewal – physical, mental, emotional and spiritual. This is no rustic cabin it is a modern facility and has a fine kitchen, dining room, gathering room, bathroom with shower and bathtub, and two bedrooms, each with a queen size bed."

When we came back on furlough from China the Shrine Board most generously gave us the gift of a night at this honeymoon type cottage. We were more than refreshed and renewed; we were enthralled, delighted and thoroughly spoiled. In fact our entire eight plus years at the Shrine of St Therese we knew it as a place of quiet rest, because there is something about the atmosphere that draws you closer to the one who created the beauty of the place, and even though our days were filled with many chores, activities and responsibilities, one glimpse out a window, one short walk across the causeway to clean the Chapel, or a brief look up as an eagle soared overhead was all it took to fill our hearts and minds with such gratitude that God had called us to *Life by the Lynn!*

ROUTINE WITHOUT A RUT

"Real Men Love to Vacuum"

One of the routine things expected of caretakers at the Shrine is vacuuming.

While retreatants vacuum the facilities before they check out, there is often the need for more thorough cleaning before the next group arrives. So vacuum cleaners were in constant use, which necessitated on-going maintenance – often before vacuuming could even begin. A broken belt, a bag needing to be emptied, a frayed electrical cord…the vacuums were not exactly *new,* in fact they had really seen better days.

We were overjoyed when a salesman introduced a new line of vacuums and the end result was the Shrine Committee determined to buy a latest model. It was one with a clear plastic container that held water so we could see how much dirt was extracted from the carpets as we cleaned. What fun! But the truth of the matter was, Bob loved vacuuming! He did not have to *see* the dirt he just loved to push the cleaner all around the rooms. I guess in comparison to jobs that took a lot of his concentration and skill, vacuuming was a "no brainer".

Especially at the end of a long hard day of plumbing problems, or electrical wiring, to take off his outdoor boots and put on slippers, plug in the cord and enjoy a relaxing walk around the lodge or a cabin was almost as good as a bubble-bath...not that Bob takes bubble-baths mind you. However, even after thirty plus years of marriage, I did not know of his innate love of vacuuming.

Bob had been super busy doing outside chores all day and at dinner he seemed really exhausted. He had an evening meeting in the valley, and the lodge still needed to be vacuumed for a group arriving early the next morning, He said as he came round the table to give me a wee kiss before leaving, "I'll take care of the lodge when I get back, I know you still have cooking to prepare for tomorrow."

I baked bread and made soup and he was still not home. So I decided to surprise him and headed over to the lodge. Back and forth I pushed the vacuum cleaner, watching as the dirt swirled around in the container, an almost mesmerizing experience. Bubbling up inside was a thrill of anticipation as I imagined Bob's hug of thanks when he got home.

I was already home and in my pj's when I heard the car come down the hill and stop outside our cozy log cabin home. I could hardly wait to tell him. "Hey, guess what? But before he could even guess, I excitedly said, "I did the vacuuming for you."

His face took on anything but a smile of appreciation.

"What's wrong?" I asked, "Aren't you pleased that you don't have to go and work some more when you are so tired?"

"Well actually; all the way home I was thinking to myself how much I was looking forward to vacuuming the lodge. Now you have already done it, and while I appreciate your thoughtfulness, *it is something I really enjoy doing*."

That was the day I learned; *Real Men Love to Vacuum!*

"Motel 6"

Being caretakers at the Shrine of St. Therese was never boring. Especially during the summer months we had an influx of visitors from all over the world along with the local regulars. Picnickers swarmed the beaches and trails around the property, school kids on Sea Week adventures clambered over rocks, and sought out hermit crabs in tide pools, tour buses brought folk from cruise ships to enjoy the beauty and serenity of the place, and take home pictures of spectacular Alaskan scenery.

The Juneau Diocese also had summer camps for Southeast Alaskan youth. They came from all over Juneau and the surrounding villages for a week of "*Fun in the Sun*," but we often thought it should be renamed "*Singin' in the Rain!*"

August, 1992 was an especially busy month as we welcomed back- to- back groups, cooking and cleaning non-stop it seemed. Bob had plenty of opportunity to be a "real man" and show his vacuuming skills. When things got almost too much for us Thomas would show up and pitch in and help, he always seemed to know just the exact moment when we were at the end of energy, he was our Barnabus. In Acts we read of this man, Barnabus, who was such an encourager of Saul and everywhere he went, we are told he assisted and helped Saul teach new believers. "He was glad and encouraged them all to remain true to the Lord with all their hearts. He was a good man, full of the Holy Spirit and faith..." Thomas was and is this kind of man.

Now, I am sure you are wondering what any of this has to do with Motel 6.

Well, don't give up keep reading.

August, 1992 we had some new lodgers, ones that reminded us of Bishop Michael's vision of expanding the reach beyond the limits of the norm and touching the community beyond our doorstep. Groups from the Alaskan Salmon Market Institute and the Juneau School Administrators tried us on for size and gave favorable reviews.

But it was the Alaska National Guard that reminded us of Motel 6.

"We'll leave the light on" was one of the most familiar slogans in the hospitality industry. It was used by Motel 6 to convey a warm invitation to travelers looking for a comfortable place to spend the night. The Alaska National Guard had chosen our "motel" to come and spend three nights. The National Guard has a worthy reputation. In nine weeks, their training program can change your life. "The challenges will be tough, but remember, you will not be asked to do anything you cannot do. Our programs train you for the career of your dreams and give you concrete skills for your resume, when employers see the National Guard on your resume they'll know they can count on you. You'll build character, explore potential and find out what you're made of."

The first day they headed out on an exercise activity, we wondered if they got lost on maneuvers as, like Motel 6, we kept the light on, in fact, all night long, for three nights. Perhaps we had misunderstood their plan. However National Guardsmen were not the only ones for whom we kept the light on, many times our "Motel 6" light was burning to bring our boarders safely home. Now, the Shrine of St. Therese, like Motel 6 and many others in the hospitality industry, we have had to adjust the welcome sign to lighting sensors and other energy saving devices. But there are many other ways besides "leaving the light on" to say welcome home. As caretakers that was our mission – to provide a hospitable welcome.

"A Rose Smelling Rosary" -or-
"A Santa Mission"

December is always a busy month, some years more than others depending on the amount of snow that falls. 1994 was a "snow" year, so we were kept on the job with the snow-blower machine and carrying wood for fires.

The Society for Creative Anachronism knights and their ladies had a great time jousting in the snow – actually I am not sure how much the ladies were enjoying the activity as they looked like they were freezing to death in their long Victorian era gowns while they watched their "knights" bat-tling opponents with blows to determine who "the best" was. We enjoyed the scene from *inside* our cozy cabin window.

But this is a tale of another interesting adventure that broke the monotony of daily duties and activities; it came in the form of a phone call.

During the summer a man from California visited the Shrine. He did some shopping in our little gift shop and bought a rosary to take home for his sister. She fell in love with it, and over the intervening weeks and months began thinking she would like to give three to friends for Christmas. She and her brother looked all over California for these spe-cial rosaries. Well they could not find any; so guess what? Late in December they finally rang us. He described what he wanted. "I need three rosaries and they *must smell like roses.*"

It was late at night when we got the phone call, and as time was short to get them to this man so his sister could mail them to her friends, I immediately went out, tromping through the snow, to the wee gift shop, which at that time was on Shrine Island. I wish you could have seen me smelling all the rosaries at 10pm by flashlight as the power had gone out. A big snowfall had brought down trees across the power lines. We had plenty of rosaries, but none of them smelled like roses.

Now it was too late to ring the Bishop, so early the next day I rang his office to see if he knew where I might find rose smelling rosaries. His secretary suggested St. Vincent DePaul. Another phone call and sure enough they had *one*! *"Yes it smells like roses, or I think it does," she said, "I have a cold."*

So off I flew to the valley on my rosary assignment, a twenty-eight mile, round trip, drive. But I had found only *one* and I needed *three* of these rose smelling rosaries.

Imagine my delight when I arrived at St Vincent DePaul and learned they had found *two* more! Now I had the three that were needed by a Santa sister in California.

Next quick trip was to the Post Office to buy a mailer. So with *Express Delivery* the rose smelling rosaries arrived in time.

Mission accomplished!

A few weeks later we had a most appreciative letter of thanks and assurance if we ever needed anything in California, just call!!

Caretakers have a varied ministry, but being Santa, delivering rose scented rosaries, was not one we recalled being in the job description!

"Braided Bread"

In February, 1993 we were having a group of Sunday school teachers from Chapel by the Lake coming for a weekend retreat, and we hoped this would be just the first of many such ecumenical outreach events.

A few days prior to their coming I got a sense that I should bake bread for their Friday night dinner. Usually I would buy the dinner breads, but I love baking bread. There is something about kneading and shaping and watching it rise. Then the fun of punching it down and watching it rise all over again. In a Mennonite cookbook, I have used for many years; it reminds us we should be *gentle* with bread.

"Be gentle when you touch bread
Let it not lie uncared for;
Unwanted
So often bread is taken for granted
There is so much beauty in bread –
Beauty of sun and soil
Beauty of patient toil
Winds and rain have caressed it
Christ often blessed it.
Be gentle when you touch bread." Author unknown.

So here I was; busy baking French bread. Not only did I bake it, but spur of the moment I decided to *braid the bread*. I made three loaves, one for each table.

The day before the dinner, Martha Zimmerman, who was the retreat speaker along with her husband, rang and said, "I just wanted to confirm a few things for the retreat. I suspect I need to ask someone to make the bread for dinner tomorrow night."

"Why?" I queried.

"Well, I want special bread as we are enacting a Sabbath meal and I want loaves of *home made French bread*."

"I just made three loaves of French bread the other day, will that do?"

"Well, that's wonderful Christie, but I need them to be *braided.*"

"Martha, you won't believe this, but I *braided the loaves!*"

We were both speechless.

The Lord had already blessed this braided Sabbath bread.

"The Bishops"

Winter months are always busy at the Shrine of St. Therese and 1990 was no exception. Lots of meals were served, many brides walked down the Chapel aisle and had their receptions in the lodge, we provided icicles from our cabin roof for a group to make ice sculptures, and we even entertained two senators on St. Valentines Day.

But for us, the highlight of the winter was a retreat in March led by Bishop Michael Kenny for the American Board of Bishops from the Lower 48. We discovered over the five days we served and cared for these elite Bishops that in fact, they were just ordinary men.

In our Sunday school class here in Kodiak, Alaska we are studying a book entitled *"Twelve Ordinary Men"*, *by John MacArthur*, who reminds us that, "while the disciples were ordinary in one sense, they were *extraordinary* in another sense. As far as their innate talents and human backgrounds are concerned, they were genuinely ordinary, and deliberately so, 'God chose the foolish things of the world to put to shame the wise, and God has chosen the weak things of the world to put to shame the things which are mighty; and the base things of the world and the things which are despised God has chosen, and the things which are not, to bring to nothing things that are, that no flesh should glory in His presence' (1st Corinthians 1:27-29 NKJV). It was only Christ's work in the disciples' lives that gave them such remarkable power and influence, so that what they became was something quite uncommon – and what they accomplished (Acts 17; 6) was something truly extraordinary."

These Bishops are esteemed and admired by many, and rightly so for the work and ministry they provided for their sheep is often *extraordinary*. But, like the disciples, it is important for all of us not to exalt them, or others in leadership positions, to a position more highly than we should, for it is the Lord they serve to whom all glory belongs.

It is so easy to be in awe of such people as Bishops, indeed I was awed by the fact that we were allowed to be in the same room and touch their robes, so to speak. I have always felt that Bishops were non-touchable. But here we were, not only in the same room, but actually having conversations with these men of God. They wandered into the kitchen, where we were cooking, to chat with us and ask about our lives as caretakers, they told jokes and we laughed together. They were ordinary men who enjoyed the food we served and appreciated the little details of service we provided, like bringing in wood to keep the fire burning – in fact they insisted on helping us carry the wood.

Perhaps you have an image in your mind of a Bishop in long flowing robes with a scepter in one hand a pile of wood in the other, well these Bishops were dressed in jeans and jumpers (sweaters) comfort and warmth came first, before robes and royalty. They were "men of the cloth" (as my father called those who are God's shepherds of His sheep), but they were down to earth, ordinary "fishermen" serving the Lord. We have a photo taken with them to prove it!

A few days after they left we had a special delivery arrive on our doorstep - a most *extraordinary* arrangement of very beautiful flowers with a wee note attached, *"Thanks* for *all* you do. From: Bishop Kenny and fellow Bishops."

Truly ordinary Bishops who blessed us in an extraordinary way!

Bishops Retreat

"God Bless the Cooks"

In the previous story I told you about the Bishop's retreat and one of the things that touched us was a habit they had at each meal before they sat down to eat.

We were in the kitchen with the food all prepared and ready to bring to the tables, just waiting for a word from Bishop Michael. The men would stand by their chairs and all together say a prayer of blessing for the food, a kind of litany. At the close of the prayer, which we could barely hear from behind closed doors in the kitchen, we would suddenly hear this *loud* announcement in unison *"And God bless the cooks"* – this was our signal to open the kitchen door and bring in the food.

It always made us smile, but more than that, it became something we began to do in our own home. As usual one of us would ask a blessing, or grace as we called it, for the meal and then Bob would say "And God bless the cooks." If he had cooked the meal, I would thank him in the same way. When we had visitors, they would ask about this unique way of thanking the cook and we would share the Bishop's Blessing story.

Some years later we were living in China and Jeri, one of my students who had become a believer, was visiting us for a holiday. As we sat saying grace before the meal, we had our usual closing, "God bless the cook" she was curious as to what that meant.

Once again we shared the "blessing" story. She went back to Beijing where she shared an apartment with Janet, another of my former students who had also become a believer. As they sat at their table having dinner, Jeri told Janet this story and together they decided to bless each other in the same manner.

A few months later, Janet's father died. Her parents were both communist party members, living in a city in southern

China, so when Janet's father passed away she invited her mother to come and live with her for a few months. Her mother spoke no English so when these young believers were speaking in English she did not understand a word they spoke.

Day after day they sat round the table together having a meal and as usual the young women would say grace, then one or the other would say, "And God bless the cook" all in English. After a few days of this the mother began to say the words as well, *in English!* Then one day she asked her daughter in Chinese, "I don't understand, what does it mean, this 'God bless the cook?'" Her daughter smiled and told her the story.

Some more time passed, as day by day the mother repeated this foreign phrase.

Then one day she said, "I know you go to a church and I would like to go with you." As this communist party mother heard the gospel stories and lived with her daughter, the Holy Spirit was at work in her heart. Until one day she said, "I would like to have Jesus in my heart."

So the Bishop's Blessing crossed the ocean, touched and changed a communist mother, who in turn was blessed as Jesus came into her heart.

"Was It A Morning Like This?"

The Shrine Board was very generous with time away for personal family needs. My Mom died on 18ᵗʰ June, 1992 and while summer is one of the busiest times of the year at the Shrine, there was no question that I should go home to Australia for her funeral. When I got back to Juneau following the trip I took time a day to reflect on the journey and wrote the following devotional.

"Was It a Morning Like This?""

"Was it a morning like this when the Son still hid from Jerusalem and Mary rose from her bed to tend the Lord she thought was dead?

Was it a morning like this when Mary walked down from Jerusalem and two angels stood at the tomb, bearers of news she would hear soon?

Did the grass sing, did the earth rejoice to feel you again?

Over and over like a trumpet underground, did the earth seem to pound?

'He is Risen?'

Over and over in a never ending round,

'He is Risen, Hallelujah! Hallelujah!'"

On Easter morning of spring 1992 our contemporary choir sang this Sandi Patti song at a sunrise service, its message nestled in my heart to bring solace to my soul many sunrises later and half a world away in the place of my youth, Australia.

Rain clouds were gathering momentum as my brothers solemnly carried our Mom's coffin out across the threshold of the picturesque, white painted country church where we had all grown up and worshipped for many years with our father as the minister. A quick prayer, "Please God don't let it rain" breathed past my lips. As we walked silently across the grass and down the gentle slope to the freshly dug grave, the sun slid out from its hiding place as if to say, "Peek-a-boo, I love you." Its winter warmth was a loving assurance the Lord had heard my plea.

As we neared the graveside, a lone piper standing a ways off on the side of the hill, played the hauntingly beautiful *"Amazing Grace"*. And suddenly God's spirit spoke in my heart oh such wonderful words, "It *was* a morning like this that Jesus rose from the dead. She (my mother) is not here *she is risen as He promised."* I wanted to shout this amazing grace-filled truth to the whole wide world, but instead I hugged my brother Bjorn's arm and whispered, "Mum is not here *she is risen!"* He hugged me back as we smiled and rejoiced together. Yet even as I rejoiced, I wondered, "What would it be like to be standing here and not know the *"Never ending round, He is Risen, Hallelujah?"*

As my brothers lowered the coffin into the cold dirt bed, the warmth of the sun and the truth of His words transformed a moment; one I had expected to be tear-filled with overwhelming loss, with a touch of comfort that rocked my hurting heart in the cradle of His love.

Was it a morning like this? My heart says a resounding *"Yes!"*

It was a morning I will *never* forget.

"911"

At the beginning of August, 1992 we had our first 911 Emergency Call since becoming caretakers.

We had a group staying at the Lodge for a number of days and while some of them were out walking around the grounds during a break, one of the women tripped on a tree root and had a nasty fall. She was in a lot of pain and it was obvious it was more than just a twisted ankle. So we rang 911 and waited with her until the ambulance arrived. I got blankets and a pillow to make her comfortable, as the medics had said not to move her. As we talked I learned she was a Presbyterian and she seemed pleased when I suggested contacting our pastor, Leon Thompson from Chapel-by-the-Lake.

There was not enough room in the ambulance for the group leader to go with Janet, the patient, so I drove him and a couple of others to the hospital. Later in the evening while talking with another group member, my husband Bob said, "Other than this I hope you have a good evening," "This" being the news that Janet had indeed broken her leg and would be in the hospital for a few days.

When Bob asked what Janet's last name was and was told, "Fitzsimmons" he replied, "We used to live in Denver, Colorado and there is a hospital there called *"Fitzsimmons Veterans Hospital"*.

"Well Bob, I'll see how smart you are," said the man, "Who was the first officer to be killed in WW1?"

"I don't know," Bob said.

"Fitzsimmons!"

They both had a good laugh.

At about 10:30pm we had a phone call from the hospital saying Janet would need to have surgery. So a message was relayed over to the folk in the Lodge. Now we waited to learn when the surgery would be scheduled and if we needed to return and bring those still at the hospital back to the Lodge.

While we were waiting someone knocked on our door, "Could you make us some popcorn please the microwave seems to be broken?" Even though the group was scheduled to leave on a Glacier Bay trip at 7am the next morning, no one seemed ready to go to bed, they were all anxious to know how Janet was doing. Popcorn seemed to be a good way to stay awake as they played cards.

Around midnight our phone rang with word that Janet was out of surgery and indeed her friends needed a ride back "home." A quick run over to the Lodge with the latest news and then off to Bartlett Memorial hospital. It had been a long day for everyone. But we were all so thankful Janet was out of surgery and seemed to be doing okay.

As the group headed out after breakfast early the next morning, we assured them we would visit Janet and get anything she needed to make her hospital sojourn as comfortable as possible. It was amazing how a 911 Emergency Call changed everyone's plans and how quickly strangers became friends. When the group returned a couple of days later we felt like family as we gave a report on the "patient" who was well on the road to complete recovery.

We discovered being Caretakers was about being the family of God!

"No Room in the Inn"

It was a cold December and a family arrived with not one animal but three.

But we had a policy, no pets indoors.

So, what to do?

They were only expected to stay for a few days, however the days became weeks, and not one, but many rules were bent to help this family in need.

Many questions were raised as a result.

What is the role of caretaker?

When are we doing our job, and when simply being a good neighbour?

When do we say no to requests for money etc., when the etc seems to be never ending?

How far should rules be bent?

We had time sheets to record how we used our time. Is it time on the job to sit and listen for two hours, or even a half hour? We lost track of the time we spent listening. As a result our whole job as Caretakers began to take shape and form as we pondered our time sheets and other questions.

When a neighbour stops by and you sense a need to "talk" or a tourist needs a listening ear, another needs a hug and time is spent, who decides when Care-taking ends and being a good neighbour begins. So often people came and we were there and time was spent. We felt it was all part of why God had called us to this place.

It was December and as we pondered the Bethlehem Babe born in a manger because there was no room in the inn, it caused us to think more deeply about our role as "Innkeepers."

There was a friend going through a divorce who needed help, potluck meals to provide, prayer retreats, wood for fires, snow to shovel, pipes to be insulated...We cleaned and cooked and answered the phone and the door, we went

Christmas caroling and all the time pondering, "No Room in the Inn." As we came and went day-by-day, helping with a wedding, shopping for groceries, baking cookies always at the edges of my mind was the family with the animals. They came knocking on our door for a band-aid, a needle and thread, sugar, wrapping paper, dimes for phone calls, letters to be mailed...an endless knocking! "No Room in the Inn" seemed like a resounding refrain that would not go away. What "room" were we being asked to provide? I think it was room in my heart!

Being a Caretaker, an Innkeeper at Christmas, took on new meaning for me that year. I discovered it is not so much *what room* we provide, as the *willingness and attitude* with which we make room. My attitude when there was no gratitude, only a knocking on the door for *more room*, was not always Christ-like.

There are still questions in terms of how best to help, but I gleaned new insight into how to make room in the inn - *open the door to your heart* and discover;

There *is* Room in the Inn!

A Crust That's Shared"

One day, a number of years before we moved to the Shrine of St Therese, I was shopping at an Arts and Crafts store when I found a beautiful embroidery kit. For some unknown reason I decided to buy two of the kits, both exactly the same.

A few years later, prior to our move to the Shrine of St Therese, my mother came from Tasmania, Australia for a visit. I had already begun working on the embroidery and one evening my mother was admiring it when I suddenly remembered that I had bought *two*. "I have another just like this one, would you like it?" I smiled. "That would be lovely," she answered.

My Mum decided to make hers into a tray cloth and I framed mine to hang on the wall. In the center of the piece were embroidered the words:

> "A Crust That's Shared
> Is Finer Food
> Than Banquet Served
> In Solitude"

We spent many evenings sitting chatting and working on our "pieces."

My Mum took hers home with her, and I had mine hanging in our dining room.

Then we moved out the road to the retreat center.

The main lodge, where many of the groups met and had their retreats, was a rustic building made out of logs. Inside the lodge, these logs shone from many years of dusting and polishing, they were beautiful and gave the room a warm cozy feeling. The main room of the lodge was divided in two with a sitting area at one end with sofas and chairs in a semi circle facing a huge wood fireplace. At the other end were tables and chairs for dining. Off to one side, on a wall close to the kitchen door, was a chest of drawers, which held cutlery and some linens etc. We used the top of this chest for a serving area with a coffee urn, mugs, sugar and creamer.

For the most part the log walls around the room were bare so after a few weeks I decided perhaps my embroidery piece would add some colour to the room, so I asked Thomas, the Director, if it would be okay for me to hang my embroidered picture on the wall above the chest of drawers. He agreed that it would make a nice addition. So, no sooner said than done!

During the course of our tenure as Caretakers we had many favourable comments as folks ponder the words and agreed with its message.

So for a season it hung on the wall in the lodge. Now we have moved and the picture hangs on the wall in another home. But no matter where we live the words remind us that it is not the food, but the fellowship round the table, that matters, or as a pastor friend said one day, "It is not the table, but what happens *at the table* that matters."

For me however, it is also a very special memory made with my Mum!

MISTAKEN IDENTITY

"An Alaskan Governor"

As we lived in the capitol city, Juneau, it was not unusual to see the Governor and other members of the Alaskan legislature around town. Many were on a first name basis with these elite leaders of our state, but for the most part I only knew them as the result of seeing their names and faces in the newspapers.

But now we were living at the Shrine of St Therese and sometimes state boards or groups would reserve an afternoon or day for meetings at the Lodge. They would ask for lunch to be provided and we would serve soup and sandwiches to democrats and republicans from around the state, they all looked alike to me, I couldn't tell the difference. Some liked meat and others were vegetarians, but they all seemed to love cookies. However, we were not always given advance notice of visiting dignitaries and this was one of those occasions.

I was busy working in the Caretakers cabin across the driveway from the Lodge and glanced out the window to see some people walking along the path towards the lodge. One of the men looked like a longtime friend. So I quickly wiped off my hands and raced out the door to greet him. Without really looking around at the group of people gathered I literally ran up the steps and threw my arms around my "friend" in a bear hug welcome.

"It is so good to see you," I said then stepped back with a big smile on my face. Immediately, another man grabbed my arm and stepped between me and the man I had hugged, I was somewhat taken aback. Then I looked up to see the rather astonished look on the face of the man I had hugged, and realized it was definitely *not* my long time friend at all, it was the *Governor of Alaska!* I was *so embarrassed!* His "security guard" had been caught "off guard" and was perhaps even *more* embarrassed than I. After all, it was his job to "*protect*" the Governor from such "*attacks*." What could I say?

The Governor was most gracious and thanked me for my "wonderful welcome."

He asked if I would be so kind as to show him the facilities as he was considering having a meeting later in the month at the Shrine. The Governor had brought his wife along with him and she asked if she might take a look in our house. "I have always thought it looked so romantic, the little cabin in the woods. Would you mind?"

Well, I was not exactly prepared for a "grand showing" of our wee dwelling place, but felt it was the least I could do after accosting her husband. It was really a lot of fun to tell her the story of the log cabin and show her through each room. She was enthralled with the "old world charm" and admired all our antique bits and pieces. By the time she and her husband left with their entourage I felt like they were indeed old friends and my embarrassing hug was forgiven.

I truly hope the security guard was also forgiven for not catching the swift of foot caretaker before she made her embarrassing *mistaken identity!*

They must have liked what they saw because we did, indeed, have a group come and it was not the last time we were to "entertain" the Governor.

"There She Is"

Especially during the summer months we had many visitors from all over the world. They came into Juneau on -

Cruise ships

Ferries

Planes

And then took sightseeing trips all around the area with the Shrine of St Therese on the list of "must see" sites.

One beautiful sunny morning I was on my knees weeding a flowerbed in front of our log cabin home which was near the retreat center parking lot when a large tour bus pulled up and stopped. A tour guide began to tell her group all about the buildings and the history of the place.

The group was made up of mostly Japanese tourists, they oohed and aahed over the beauty and all the time cameras clicked.

I kept on weeding.

Suddenly a man shouted to his companions,

"There she is, there she is, over there in the garden, it's Mother Teresa!"

Before I could get off my knees and explain the mistake,

Cameras were focused

Pictures were taken

And the tour guide was ushering everyone back on the bus!

Later when I told my husband of the incident, we both laughed.

We could just imagine those tourists back home in Japan showing their family and friends; "Look, we got a picture of Mother Teresa in Alaska."

How could they make such a mistake? For a number of reasons perhaps:

- The sign at the entrance to the center said, "*Shrine of St Therese*"
- It would seem logical therefore that Mother Teresa might live there.
- Maybe they only knew the name and very little about where she lived etc.
- Probably they had never met Mother Teresa, seen her picture, or knew how she spelled her name.

However, regardless of the reasons, it was amazing, just because *one person* announced, "There she is, Mother Teresa" a crowd of people believed!

Makes me wonder –

If someone said, "There He is; that's Jesus," would we know?

Would we recognize Him - if indeed it was Him?

How would we know for sure?

More importantly, would we believe?

A BOAT

"The Libby"

O ff to the side of the Caretakers cabin and down near the beach, we noticed a boat somewhat buried in tall grass and weeds. So one day in our spare time we went investigating. We discovered it to be "The Libby" a stainless steel boat that looked like it had been on some pretty rough trips, if the dents and scratches along the sides and bow, and the broken glass panel in the wheel house window were any indication.

I have a book *"Cradle of the Storms", by Bernard R. Hubbard S.J."* who was also known to many around the world as *"The Glacier Pries,t"* a nickname he earned in the 1920's while a Jesuit in theology studies in Innsbruck, Austria, because whenever possible he went on expeditions in the Tyrolean Alps. Although he was a priest, it was his annual Alaskan expeditions from 1927 until he died in 1962 that made him a legend.

According to an article I read, he explored Alaska by foot, dogsled, umiak (a walrus-hide boat) pontoon plane and Coast Guard Cutter. Now we discovered, this somewhat battered boat down by the beach, was used by this amazing man to travel around Alaskan waters, especially the Taku Ice Cap, a seventy-five mile expanse of treacherous tides and ice flows. Frances Talbot in the preface to the book *"Cradle of the Storm"* says, "On a former trip, his wooden boats were smashed and split against the rocks." So perhaps this is why he took the next trip in this stainless steel boat "The Libby".

"Half the year the highest paid lecturer in the world, the other half a wanderer among treacherous craters and glaciers" was the way *Literary Digest* described Father Bernard Hubbard. When Father Hubbard began his Alaskan adventures it was before *"The Last Frontier"* was even a state. To an explorer like Hubbard, the Alaskan wilderness was just the kind of challenge that lured him, like gold did those who came north seeking their fortunes.

According to author Jeff Kunkel, this amazing man, "Began each day with mass, carried 100 pounds of scientific and photographic equipment on his back, and said the rosary when confronted by danger...with the coming of World War 11, Hubbard consulted with the armed forces, befriended military officers, and entertained Alaskan troops. After the war, he photographed the devastated Jesuit communities of Europe and the construction of the Al-Can Highway."

Father Hubbard – The Glacier Priest, died of a stroke in 1962 while robing for mass.

I wonder what tales his boat, *The Libby*, could tell had it a tongue.

I am sure they would keep folks sitting round a beach bonfire for hours.

HERE COMES THE BRIDE
Introduction

Michael Phillips and Judith Pella have co-authored a number of books one is
"The Stonewycke Legacy" series.

In the introduction to one of the books they put in a nutshell a piece of "happily ever-after" that is often overlooked.

"Their (Allison and Logan, two of the characters in the story) coming together cannot be viewed as an end, but rather as the beginning of an on-going journey...Certainly a deep joy has its part in this journey, but a truly God-divined path will be richly filled with trials as well.

The long-haul character of life's most meaningful relationships and experiences is often overlooked by our short-sighted vision which views only the now. We make decisions lightly, little considering the day-by-day lifetime of dedication necessary to carry them out. Nor do we see the unavoidable adversities which will build inner resiliency and strength of character that enables us to persevere in those aspects of life to which we have pledged ourselves.

In no two areas of life do our decisions and surface expectations run aground from lack of awareness of the long-haul than in marriage and spiritual dedication...neither commitment to marriage nor to God comes easy. The decision can be made in a moment. Living out the commitment to that decision, that requires something altogether different than a burst of enthusiasm.

All husbands and wives – and all Christians – must eventually pass through the same refining process if they are to discover what true commitment is – to one another and to the Lord. That process of growth is the soil out of which maturity is able to blossom."

So the following stories about weddings and honeymoons at the Shrine of St Therese are just the beginnings of their on-going journeys and we hope and pray each and every one of these couples relationships have indeed matured and blossomed over the intervening years.

"The Brides Room"

Out on Shrine Island, the beautiful stone chapel is a favorite place for weddings. Brides come from all over Alaska and even from the Lower 48 states to be married in this historic setting.

One of the very pleasant responsibilities we had as caretakers was to prepare the chapel for these weddings and to assist the bridal parties as requested.

Early on we discovered that there was only a small gift shop area behind the sacristy where brides could change. So we went searching for a better arrangement.

At the front of the building we discovered a wee room where the bell was rung.

It was rather musty and dusty from lack of use. So we asked if we could clean it up and make it into a Bridal changing room. Permission granted was all we needed to begin the transformation.

I discovered an old picture of the first bridal couple married at the Shrine of St Therese, Walter and Helen Sebesta on 27th November, 1941 and they returned for a celebration and renewal of their vows in 1989. So, along with the picture, I got together some other pieces of memorabilia and had it framed to put on the wall in this wee room.

Next I decorated a large box with pretty fabric and gathered together some items I thought all brides might find helpful on their special day – things like; Advil and Tylenol, Kleenex, thimble and thread, buttons, a pair of nylons, hair spray, nail polish, Talcum powder, safety pins, A garter (just in case it had been forgotten) It was fun to go shopping and think about what a bride or groom might need at the last minute. I am sure readers can give some more suggestions to add to the box! Following each wedding we also had to remember to replenish the box for the next bridal party.

In August, 1990 we had five weddings, and one of the brides chose to have her reception in the Lodge. As she walked across the causeway after the ceremony in the Chapel I overheard her say to her newly wed husband, "I think I like being married, this is great, I've never done this before, I think it is forever!"

One dear bride came and set up the day prior to the wedding with candles and flowers. During the evening someone came and took three of the candles from the candelabra and lit two others. By the time we went out for our usual Chapel closing later in the evening the candles were 2/3 burned. It was very upsetting for all concerned and caused us to ask some questions about the need to lock the door when brides set up early.

Some brides were more stressed than others, but sometimes it was the father of the bride, like the one who, after the rehearsal, hid the combination lock to the brides changing room. He was no where to be found the day of the wedding and the bride was ready to get changed. When finally found he said, "I hid it because I just thought you might not be here and we would need it to open the door."

Sometimes it was the Caretakers who became stressed. This was a lesson learned, and from then on we kept the lock where we knew *we* could find it!

A Limo of a Different Kind

April, 1993 began with a leadership retreat led by Sister Joan and ended with one led by Father Weber. In-between there were many retreats.

We also had a Shrine Work-Party day, and because we had exceptional spring weather, flowers were planted and humming bird feeders were hung.

Hardly a day passed that we did not have fishermen and tourists on the scene.

It was also a perfect month for weddings!

We had four weddings and a couple of them were rather unique and worthy of note. One we were not present to observe but Bishop Michael related the event.

The bride was piped (bagpipes) across the causeway and into the chapel. Following the ceremony she and the bridal party were piped back across the causeway. Kilts were the order of the day and worn by the groom and his best man. Bishop Michael Kenny had a special tartan stole provided for him to wear at the ceremony. He smiled as he told the tale. I think he must have enjoyed the pipes, being of Irish descent. Being a Scot, it was a wedding I wish we *had* seen. It reminded me of my own wedding day and my youngest brother piping me into the church and also following the wedding ceremony. For Scots, the *skirl of the pipes* is a most stirring thing and *definitely* the most wonderful way to be wed!

The other wedding of interest attracted a lot of attention, especially from tourists and other visitors around at the time the bride and groom walked across the causeway from Shrine Island following the wedding ceremony. They were having their reception at another venue, so transport was awaiting their departure at the parking lot. However this was not the anticipated limousine!

As the guests gathered around the bridal pair and began to throw birdseed, the bride took off her veil and handed it to her mother in return for a winter jacket which she proceeded to put on over her full length wedding dress. She hugged her Mom, and then taking the veil put it back on her head. Her newly wed husband also donned a winter coat and then handed his bride - guess what? *A helmet!*

We watched incredulously as she put it on *over the top of her veil* - it fit just perfectly as she nonchalantly snapped the strap under her chin, then with the helmet in place, we watched in amazement as she bent down, gathered the voluminous skirt up above her knees and hopped on to the "limo of a different kind" – *a motor bike!*

She reached her arms around her bridegroom's waist and before we could catch our breath - vroom-vroom they were off up the road in a cloud of dust!

Wow! It took a moment for everyone to recover before applause broke out.

Life by the Lynn was never dull!

Honeymoon Haven

The Post Office was always a favorite place for retreats, but we discovered early on, it was also a popular place for honeymoons.

We enjoyed fixing the "honeymoon suite" for Tim Spangler and his Polish bride. They seemed most appreciative. Theirs was a unique wedding with a *dog as the ring-bearer*. We jokingly asked Bishop Kenny if we had permission for a dog to be in the Chapel. He said, "From the highest authority." Then he thought for a moment and smiled,

"Well, at least from the highest *local* authority."

So it was that the dog walked down the aisle carrying the ring, to the delight of all the guests gathered for the ceremony.

But this was not the first time we prepared the honeymoon suite. Our first honeymooners were Peter and Sandy Metcalfe. I was so excited to be preparing for a honeymoon that I asked Thomas if we could do something special to make the Post Office more inviting for a young couple just married. I simply couldn't imagine them sleeping in bunk beds on their honeymoon.

So Bob helped me fix the mattresses on the floor into a large queen size bed, then I headed for town and bought some new sheets and towels, candles and flowers etc and had such fun decorating the honeymoon suite for this young couple. Candy kisses on the pillows were the final touch!

Our prayers for them to have a sunny weekend were answered. Praise the Lord!

I recently wrote Peter and Sandy and asked if they would be willing to tell their honeymoon story for my book, they most graciously agreed.

So enjoy the romance of -

A proposal
A wedding
And a honeymoon!

A HONEYMOON AT THE POST OFFICE
BY
PETER AND SANDY METCALF

"A cold snap had brought an early fall, but with it clear weather, Sandy and I were at the Turner lake cabin just above Taku Inlet, about a 30 mile floatplane ride from the Juneau airport. It was the second weekend of September, 1992. I had been sure to rent the original Turner Lake cabin, a stone and log cottage built by the Civilian Conservation Corps in the 1930's, a romantic cabin made ever more so by the stunning scenery and the gorgeous early fall weather. A full moon reflected on the surface of Turner Lake the evening I proposed. Although we had been dating for over five years, Sandy seemed genuinely surprised. Before accepting, she insisted that if I meant it – I had suggested that *maybe we should get married* – I ask properly, I did!

We set the wedding date for 30th October of that year, just seven weeks hence.

The short schedule reduced our options, but the new visitor's center at the DIPAC Hatchery was available and we took it. With the help of friends and family the public space was festooned with banners and arrayed throughout were dozens of candles, most fitted in candleholders custom-made by a close friend. The cleverly arranged decorations magically converted the industrial setting into a temporary cathedral. Friends organized an impromptu band that provided music for our wedding and the festivities that followed. The only flaw in the arrangement was that by the time Sandy and I had received all the congratulations, the delicious spread of locally harvested salmon, halibut, shrimp and all the other dishes, had largely disappeared.

After midnight we were able to make a graceful exit from DIPAC, but our car required some attention, our windshield had to be cleared of shaving cream-inscribed wedding announcements, and I wasn't about to depart with a stream of inflated condoms trailing in our wake. But soon enough we were on our way for a weekend honeymoon at the shrine of St Therese.

We had a trip planned to Belize, but that was scheduled for January. For our first days together as husband and wife, I had suggested to Sandy that we rent a cabin at the Shrine where my parents had honeymooned. Inquiring with the Loney's, who resided on site, we rented the "Post Office" cabin for the first weekend of our marriage.

Only our headlights illuminated the narrow access road. As we pulled up to the Post Office, flickering candlelight from inside invited us through the glass framed door. Stars shone brightly as a north wind rustled the tree limbs above us and sent saltwater waves rolling up the gravel beach. I swept Sandy into my arms and we crossed the threshold into a beautifully decorated cabin stocked with a weekend's worth of food; arrangements made by our friends, Rachel and Shari. As we learned later Christie and Bob Loney decorated the cabin. It was charming, cozy, comfortable, and our midnight meal made all the more delicious by our hunger.

That weekend we were blessed by beautiful late fall weather. During our walks out to the island and the church I reflected on my parents' honeymoon at the same place 45 years earlier.

In June, 1947 my parents, Vernon Marvin and Patricia (McAlister) Metcalf, were married at the Cathedral of the Nativity of the Blessed Virgin at 5th and Gold Streets in Juneau. My father, a sheet metal worker, was the wage earner, and as he told me much later, he was just as broke then as he was when he had nine kids. In any event, honeymoons that involved travel were exceptional in those days. My parents chose the Shrine, a fixture in my mother's young life.

During her youth, my mother and her three sisters participated in summer camps organized by the Catholic Daughters of America (CDA). There is a family photo of my mother, one of a pyramid of girls, in front of a row of wall tents on the edge of the lawn at the Shrine with the newly built lodge in the background. The year was 1936.

In contrast to the pile of smiling, healthy young girls, in the background a hand-lettered sign reads "CDA Concentration Camp" illustrated by a backward Nazi swastika. Truly a sign of the times (It should be said that in 1936, such camps were a newsreel curiosity and had not acquired the dreadful connotations soon to come.)

In later life, as my mother presided over the family picnics we held so often near the very spot she and her friends had erected their tents, we would hear stories of summer camps at the Shrine. My mother proudly recalled her role, and that of the other CDA girls, in hauling rocks, two girls to the wheelbarrow, for the causeway and stone cathedral.

By the time Sandy and I married, both our parents had passed on. But on those first days of our marriage, Sandy and I walked the very grounds where my parents had begun theirs. Thanks to the caretakers our time together was spent in the cozy confines of a beautifully appointed cabin, and due to the time of year, virtually undisturbed by visitors."

Romance is Still Alive

Thanksgiving weekend 1994 found us with a full house at the Lodge and the Post Office plus a Chapel wedding. Not only that, but we had a record snow fall for the month.

Bob was very busy climbing ladders to replace light bulbs in the Chapel, finishing a box to cover the water pipes beside our house so they would not freeze (this was a *high priority*), fixing broken chairs, taking care of plumbing problems in four bedrooms in the Lodge before the big group arrived.

And of course shoveling snow every day! In fact we both shoveled our way over to work at the Lodge and Post Office one day, and by the time we were done with our chores we had to shovel our way home again!

Into the midst of this busyness we were asked to be witnesses at a wedding.

I wonder how often Caretakers, or anyone for that matter, get to be best-man and bridesmaid for people they have never met before.

It was a very small wedding:

The bride and groom

A photographer from F-Stop

Two violinists

The minister

And Bob and me!

They had been childhood sweethearts but then they went their separate ways.

They both got married and had children.

Now, without spouses, they had met up again at a recent High School reunion and youthful love was reignited!

He had lived in Juneau many years ago and loved the Shrine of St Therese so they decided this was the place they wanted to tie the knot. So they flew into Juneau the day before the wedding and came out to the Shrine to meet with us and discuss the arrangements. Then out of the blue; "Would you be willing to stand with us and be our witnesses, we would really appreciate if you would do that for us?" We were delighted to say, "Yes."

Everything went according to plan except the bride was so excited that she forgot her bouquet and left it in the pew at the back of the Chapel - But none-the-less it was a very lovely ceremony!

They spent their first night at Grandma's Bed and Breakfast in the valley and the next day they flew to Anchorage and drove to Wasilla to surprise their unsuspecting family with the news; "We got married!"

Yes –

Romance is still alive!

A Surrey with a Fringe on Top

These two had been our friends for some years; in fact we knew the bride and her family from a previous marriage and were very sad when they got a divorce. However it was not long before we became good friends with the man who was to become her second husband. They decided early on in their dating that they wanted "to keep themselves pure" until their wedding day. So it was, that one Sunday we had a phone call from Barbara asking if we would "chaperone" them that afternoon because they wanted to bake some cookies at Phillip's apartment. Now this was no teenager baking date, these were people in their mid 30's or more, so you can imagine it felt a little strange to be asked to be chaperones. But it proved to be a lot of fun and we spent the afternoon together drinking tea and chatting together.

When I began to write this book I remembered their very special wedding day and the reception at our house at the Shrine of St Therese which we had offered to host, so I wrote to Phillip and Barbara asking for permission to tell their story. Indeed, I asked if they would like to write an account of that day for me to include; so here it is.

"For us the name of the Shrine's "Caretaker's Cabin" was particularly appropriate. Christie and Bob spent most of the year, leading up to our wedding, *caring* for us. Phillip and I met in a Sunday school class led by Christie, and learned more about each other in the prayer group that Christie and Bob invited us to join. Christie and Bob had even acted as chaperones for some of our dates, so when these *"Caretakers"* offered to host the wedding reception at the Shrine, their loving gesture was gratefully accepted.

Both of us were starting over after difficult marriages, and most of my (Barbara's) family was coming to Alaska for the first time, so the beauty of the Shrine and affordability of the Post Office cabin provided the perfect solution.

The reception was pot luck, but the groom (Phillip) made the wedding cake and the cozy Caretakers cabin held all the guests. Friends in Hawaii sent gorgeous leis for everyone in the wedding party and the rainforest provided the final blessing by holding off on its main product; rain!

At the high point of the reception celebration, Bob and Christie called to us to join them on the steps outside where we were surprised to hear about a Shrine "tradition." Waiting on the bottom of the steps outside was a wheelbarrow decked out to look like a surrey with a fringe on top. A wooden frame held a white canopy and the barrow was lined with pillows and a soft sheepskin from New Zealand. Apparently, from what we were told, the marriage would be a blessed and successful one if the groom could push his bride up the hill on the dirt access road. The "groom" was game and once I the "bride" managed to get myself into the "surrey with the fringe on top" none too gracefully I might add, off we went to cheers and laughter and many photographs.

At the top of the hill, Phillip declared that it only seemed fair that his bride should give him a ride back down. More hoots and hollers ensued when we rounded the corner and came in sight. I was wearing 3" heels and as the wheelbarrow surrey gained momentum I promptly lost control and dumped my bridegroom out into the dirt."

It was a one time "tradition" that our daughter, Sharon, and son-in-love Bob, who were home from college, helped us to create. As far as we know this "tradition" has never been repeated. After the wedding guests left, we had fun getting rides in the "surrey."

We still chuckle at this memory.

CREATIONS CREATURES

The Shrine Cat

Sometimes friendships only last a wee while and then again there are those that last through thick and thin for many years. Our friendship with Stan and Dellene Love and their family is of the latter kind. In fact, not only are we friends with the whole family, but we also enjoyed their cat, Boomer!

When the family was moving south to Oregon they decided not to take Boomer who was not only getting up in years but was also very much an outdoor cat. They would be living in an apartment in a city where a cat would not be able to roam around outside.

So Dellene rang me one day and asked, "Would you be willing to take Boomer?"

At first we were not sure, as the Shrine Board had a policy of no animals inside the Caretakers house, or any of the facilities for that matter, but when Dellene explained that Boomer would be more than happy to be outside and roam the grounds, we said we would ask for permission. No worries! So Boomer came to live with us.

Boomer had quite a personality and for the most part did not like to be petted. But after some weeks he began to venture closer and rub his body alongside my legs and purr in a more friendly fashion. But he would have nothing to do with any of the retreat visitors or tourists and would disappear at first sight under the front porch, where he usually slept, or wander off into the woods.

When Bob and I would go to the valley for shopping or to meet with friends we always tried to return by 9pm to give Boomer his goodnight treat and pat. Almost without exception Boomer went to bed around 9pm. If we were late coming home from an outing – he left a personal poop "message" on the doorstep which clearly expressed his disgust; we could almost hear his meow – "You're late again!"

In January, 1991 war broke out in the Middle East.

Bishop Michael Kenny called for a Peace Vigil which was originally set to be held at the Shrine of St Therese and then moved to the valley making it more accessible at a time of critical need for prayer.

However a group of people came and spent the night at the Lodge. They signed up for an hour at a time so all night long there would be someone praying in the Chapel.

For some unexplained reason Boomer decided the people going back and forth in the middle of the night across the causeway to pray in the Chapel needed an escort. So all night long he would sit on a step at the Lodge and when someone came out he would walk beside them across the causeway. Then he waited on the Chapel steps until they came out and would walk them back to the Lodge again. Back and forth he went providing his comforting presence in the dark night.

I sometimes wonder if he knew it was a Peace Vigil and this was his way of participating! In any case - that night Boomer became the Shrine Cat!

The Shrine Cat – Part Two

The following winter was very cold with lots of snow and the driveway was unusually icy. One Sunday morning we had been to the church service at

Chapel-by-the-Lake in Auke Bay and were driving very carefully down the icy hill to the parking area beside our home, when I shouted out "Stop Bob, there is an animal on the road."

We jumped out of the car and there, stretched out across the driveway, was Boomer. Who knows how long he had been there, but at least 3-4 hours because we left home around 8am and it was now after 1pm. We felt for a pulse and any sign of life but he was frozen stiff and dead. He was "family" and we were devastated!

Later, we sat at the table trying to decide what we should do with his body.

The ground was too frozen to bury him in the woods and so Bob suggested we take him to the edge of the ocean and let the tide take him out to sea. I just could not do that. The water was icy cold and even though I knew he was dead I simply couldn't bear the thought of just putting him in the freezing water and letting him drift out beyond our sight. Bob said, "I will take care of him and we will bury him in the woods in the spring."

Boomer was dead and I really missed his eccentric ways, the place seemed empty without him and especially in the evening I missed our "goodnight Boomer" routine.

One day, a few weeks later, we decided to invite friends over for the evening and I went to the chest freezer on our front porch to get some meat to thaw for dinner, inside right on top of everything was a brown paper package, "Oh, how nice, someone has brought us some salmon, maybe I will change the menu and have fish for dinner" I thought. I removed the wrapping paper and a wail of pain filled the air,

"Oh no – it is Boomer!" I went running through the house crying, "Bob, how could you, you put Boomer in the *freezer* and it is *so-o-o-o* cold."

I am sure you are laughing.

How ridiculous -

Boomer was dead.

But Bob understood and just hugged me as I cried out my grief and loss.

By the time spring came and the ground was thawed enough to dig in the woods we had a Boomer burial.

The Shrine Cat was laid to rest -

I was finally ready to say goodbye,

And the ground was not so *cold!*

"The Grandstand View" By Scarlett A. Loney

The Grand Stand View

Our log cabin home was comfortable and cozy with many windows out of which we enjoyed God's amazing creation. No matter where we looked we had a view;

Water vistas,

Forest green,

Rocky beaches,

The Lynn Canal - (Often called "The Breadbasket" by fishermen, who would come in their boats and spend the day catching their supper.)

And -

An incredible, uninterrupted view of the snow-capped Chilkat mountain range on the opposite shores of the Inside Passage waters of the Lynn Canal. It truly was an idyllic place to live!

One of the kitchen windows near my desk looked out across the access road which came down from Glacier highway, past our log cabin, and into the parking lot of the Shrine of St Therese. Across the road were the Lodge and a vista of the beach beyond, but right in close to the house, at the side of the road, were some large evergreen trees in a semi circle. Inside the circle area was a large scooped out area in the dirt, probably made as the result of winter snow removal. In any case it looked a lot like a sports arena.

Early one morning as I was working on some papers preparing the monthly Caretakers report, I happened to be looking out the window when two weasels, sporting their brownish summer coats, arrived on the scene. (Weasels have a very beautiful white ermine coat in winter)

I watched in fascination as these two entered the "arena" area and walked around and around eyeing each other across the dugout dirt space. After some minutes they took up positions in the middle of the "arena" and, to what seemed to me like some unheard gunshot announcing the beginning of their sport, began to go at each other with a vengeance.

As if this was not enough entertainment -

Out of nowhere, a murder of crows arrived; they crowded above in the tree top stadium bleacher branches. It was absolutely hilarious! The caw-cawing of the crows seemed to get louder and louder as the weasels battled in the arena below. It was very evident the crows had chosen sides and were caw-cawing their support from their bleacher branches for their chosen weasel.

The louder the crows got, the more the weasels went at each other. Then, almost without any warning the fight was over with no apparent winner. We watched as two rather beaten looking weasels took off in different directions; to lick their wounds I suspect.

And the crows -

They flew off to "caw" another day!

"Mi Casa Es Su Casa"

Have you ever watched a mother squirrel teaching her babies how to jump from branch to branch? It is fascinating. I am not sure how the mommy squirrels know when their babies are old enough to begin the jumping process, but they seem to begin way too young for what appears to me as a rather brutal lesson.

Our youngest son, David, and I watched for almost an hour as a mommy squirrel began pushing, with her nose, a teeny tiny wee squirrel, she pushed her baby closer and closer to the edge of the roof and then as though she knew exactly how far it was from the roof ledge to the nearby tree she gave a big shove and the poor we thing fell spread eagled down, down, down towards the ground hitting branches and twigs on the way, seemingly unable to stop, until thud, the fall ended on the ground some thirty or more feet below.

But this was not the end of the lesson.

She had about six or more wee ones and one by one they were pushed along the ledge and shoved over the edge. When all the babies were on the ground the mother squirrel herself jumped into the tree and scrambled to the ground where she picked up a baby in her mouth and climbed all the way back up to the roof where she deposited it in safety. Back down she went for the next one and repeated the process until all her babies were safe and sound.

Now, I thought, she would be exhausted from all this exercise and take a nap.

Not so! The daily lesson had just begun.

She began the process all over again; push, shove, and plop, jump, pick up and climb again. Round and round she went teaching these little ones the art of jumping. I don't know how many times it took before the wee one would get up enough courage to go to the edge and jump of their own volition, but if the mother squirrel had any say the babies really had no choice in the matter.

However, while squirrels held a great fascination for us, we were not at all happy having them as *full time boarders* in our house.

They left their messes everywhere.

They chewed on electrical wiring in the attic, a grave concern as a fire hazard.

We had to throw out dry goods like flour, sugar, oatmeal etc.

They seemed to be everywhere!

One morning I was busy baking in the kitchen when *plop* a squirrel landed right on the counter next to my baking bowl barely missing landing in the batter. Very funny! But "funny" lasted only a second, *something had to be done!* So off Bob went to the hardware store and came home with a *live trap!*

The very next morning we came out to get breakfast and there on the counter *inside* the trap was a squirrel and on the counter beside the trap door was *another squirrel*. I don't know how we had not heard the commotion from the bedroom as they were chattering back and forth very obviously trying to figure out how to get out of the trap.

Thus began many trips, over thirty, out the road beyond the Shrine of St Therese and across a river to drop off the squirrels, with the hope they would not find their way back to the Caretaker's Cottage again but enjoy a tree hollow home in the woods.

The next step was to find their entry holes.

We lived in a log cabin and the holes seemed endless.

But each one we found we stuffed with insulation material and then boarded them up. This seemed to work until we heard a very distracted mother squirrel chattering away to her babies who had somehow got trapped *inside*. So what could we do but open up the hole and let her get in again. Unfortunately she seemed to be in no hurry to come out of her home in our house. But we kept filling in holes anyway. However, no matter how many holes we filled there always seemed to be another.

Then winter came and the squirrels were very happy with their cozy habitat.

But the trips out the road continued as squirrel after squirrel enjoyed peanut butter treats and were caught in the live trap. Only this time Bob, feeling sorry to be disturbing their winter hideaway, took some spruce cones and wee pieces of torn up blanket to help them keep warm and fed until spring.

We never did solve the squirrel habitation problem – maybe they had heard and believed the words of a 60's song sung by Bing Crosby;

"Mi Casa Es Su Casa – My house is your house."

What do you think?

A Lesson in Lobtailing

Many tourists come from all over the world and take cruise ships and ferries up the *Inside Passage* to Alaska. One of their favourite things to do is take a whale watching tour. These mammals are simply amazing creatures. Did you know the Blue whale is the largest animal that has ever existed on earth? It is in fact larger than any of the dinosaurs were! The Blue whale can grow to be 94 feet long, that's the height of a nine story building. These amazing mammals eat 4 tons of tiny krill *every day,* now that's a lot of food to find. But the smallest whale is only 8.5 feet long and called the Dwarf sperm whale. Still pretty big in my book as I am only 5'2".

Whales belong to a species called Cetaceans which include whales, dolphins and porpoises. There are over 75 species of Cetaceans and of these; whales are divided into two groups; Toothed and Baleen. As you might have guessed Blue whales are Baleen whales. Baleen whales have two blowholes. Whether you are out on an Alaskan State Ferry, a whale-watching tour, fishing boat or private pleasure craft, everyone keeps their eyes peeled for white spray that blows up in the air, a sign of a spouting whale. Keep watching and you might see the body of the whale as he roles over and over moving along on his journey. Sometimes the whales leap out of the water and almost their entire body becomes visible. This is called breaching. Whales are very acrobatic animals and often do this simply for fun or to loosen skin parasites. As they come back down they slap their tails on the water and the sound can be heard for miles around.

Killer whales and Shortfin Pilot whales are very fast and can swim at speeds up to 30 miles per hour (48 kph). Sometimes whales pop their heads out of the water somewhat like a submarine periscope, just to take a look around, this is called Spyhopping.

Much has been written about whales singing. A humpback's song can last as long as 30 minutes. The whale's song is thought to be used as a means of courting, and also to keep track of baby whales. Their song can be heard for miles underwater.

Living at the Shrine of St Therese we had a front seat view of whales all year long, although they usually left to migrate south to warmer waters for the winter we sometimes had sightings in close to the shore during winter months. We watched toothed whales one day, in the small bay close to the Lodge, as they circled around together trapping sea lions unable to escape as they formed their "net".

But I will never forget the day I watched a mother whale and her baby, they were almost close enough to reach out and touch from the rocky shore of Shrine Island.

They were Lobtailing!

How fascinating to see the very large tail of the mommy whale sticking straight up out of the water and the teeny wee tail just barely showing. It seemed as though the mother was showing the baby how to "lob." Her huge whale tail came up out of the water and then with a mighty whack it came crashing down hitting the water like a large flat board, the sound reverberating in the air like thunder. Then the baby whale, imitating the mother, whacked its wee tail in similar fashion. Over and over again they practiced Lobtailing together. I could almost hear the mother say, "That's it, good work. Now try and make it louder, whack harder this time!" No one seems to know exactly the purpose of Lobtailing; some say it may be used as a warning system. But from what I could see it just looked like a lot of fun! Can't you hear a Mommy say to her youngster,

"Hey, let's go Lobtailing today!"

Mother Marmot

At the Shrine of St Therese there was always something going on in the animal kingdom. Every season of the year was different and fascinating. It was a veritable zoo.

We had bears, weasels, land otters, seals, squirrels, marmots, whales, porpoise, salmon, eagles, humming birds, crows, hedgehogs, dogs and cats and even pet hamsters that a visitor brought one day. Life by the Lynn was never dull.

I am reminded of one of my favourite hymns; "All things bright and beautiful, all creatures great and small, all things wise and wonderful, the Lord God made them all. He gave us eyes to see them and lips that we might tell..."

So let me tell you about one of God's amazing creatures; the marmot.

According to Wikipedia "marmots are a genus, Marmota, of squirrels. These cuddly looking furry creatures have short stocky legs and very sharp claws with which they burrow down into the ground and make their home. Marmots are almost entirely vegetarian; they are very active in the day-time (diurnal) and hibernate in the winter.

Very soon after they come out of their burrow home in the spring, they mate and have their babies. About a month after she gets pregnant a mother marmot gives birth to anywhere from 4-6 babies. Marmots usually produce every year. Most marmots are very social creatures and very protective of one another. At the sight or sound of danger they let out a piercing, high pitched whistle sound to communicate with one another. I am not sure if this is also used to keep track of babies as well as just an aspect of their social networking, rather like "texting" maybe.

One spring we had a very pregnant marmot come calling.

I watched as she slowly lumbered along the path from the beach and into our garden area. Ever so slowly she came closer and closer to the house and finally I watched in amazement as she managed to get herself up a step and then another until she was sitting right outside our French glass doors into the living room. There was barely room for her swollen body on the narrow step as she began banging with her nose on the glass.

I wonder; had she seen me from the beach standing at the window watching? Did she decide our soft carpet might be a perfect place to have her babies? I have no idea what she had in mind, but it was evident she wanted to come in as she continued to announce her presence at the glass door. Unfortunately I have not had training as a marmot midwife, and it was not part of the Caretakers job description, so after quite some time mother marmot sadly gave up. She managed to get herself off the steps and waddled slowly off into the woods behind the house to have her babies.

I have often wondered what might have happened had the French doors been open. I guess we will never know!

A REAL THANKSGIVING

Come and See

Thanksgiving in America is celebrated a little differently than the way with which I grew up. In the British Isles and Commonwealth countries we celebrate a Harvest Thanksgiving but it is primarily a worship service with the sanctuary all decorated with sheaves of grain and bounty of the field and fruit trees as well as baked goods. As people come to worship they bring their offerings from the harvest and lay them at the altar. When the service of thanks to God is concluded the food etc is taken and distributed to the poor as well as to hospital patients and orphanages. There is no great feasting in the homes of the nations nor is there a national holiday. For me the memory is one of a special worship service and singing some of my favourite hymns like "We plough the fields and scatter the good seed on the land…"

My first Thanksgiving in America was celebrated in a hospital in Denver, Colorado the day after our first child was born, a son whom we named Andrew.

When my breakfast tray was brought to me on Thanksgiving Day morning I noticed a piece of paper with the words across the top "Five Grains of Corn at Thanksgiving" Underneath was the story of the first Thanksgiving celebrated in Plymouth Colony the year after the most unbelievable hardship. It told of sickness, starvation and death that took nearly half of the pilgrim population. Food was so scarce that they near the end of winter "the bread-stuff consisted of a ration of five grains of corn per person for each meal. At last came spring, followed by a good crop season in summer…there was an abundance of corn, squash, beans, barley, dried wild fruits and the like so that there was a supply for winter and to spare. Governor Bradford proclaimed a Harvest Festival of three days to begin with a religious service."

The story relates how the tables were all set as though for a feast but when the people came they found only *five grains of corn* on each plate. They colonists all remembered immediately the previous year's hardship. Elder Brewster spoke about the meaning of the five grains, symbols of want and the feast they would later have and suggested that the difference was to be credited wholly to the goodness of God.

Thanksgiving Day in America was birthed as the result of recognizing the goodness of God in the midst of daily life. Yes, many died but many survived and a nation began to grow and prosper by giving thanks. For many years this is how Thanksgiving was celebrated, but slowly, down through the years, many have forgotten and Thanksgiving Day is simply a day off work, a holiday, a day of feasting. However in the Christian community we still take time to gather for worship and then go home for a feast.

Ever since my experience in the hospital, that first Thanksgiving, we have always had five grains of parched field corn set at each plate. We have a time of sharing as each person tells of five blessings of God from the previous year. I always give a copy of "Five Grains of Corn" to each guest and in this way the traditions of that first Thanksgiving continue to be shared. Then the feasting begins!

Our first Thanksgiving at the Shrine of St Therese was no different except it was held in a log cabin. I had the table all set with our handmade lace tablecloth, our silver cutlery and fine china all arranged at each place, a floral centerpiece and candles ready to be lit on the following day – Thanksgiving Day.

We had oil lamps lit and a fire burning in the wood stove as I began to walk round the table placing five grains of corn on each plate when there was a knock at the door. It was Tom Satre, the chair of the Shrine Board.

He and his family have a tradition of celebrating Thanksgiving at the Post Office Cabin and they were getting all settled in for the night when he walked across the parking lot to bring us special greetings from the Board. So we invited him into our cosy wee cabin. He immediately began to admire our table and the way the room looked in the lamplight. "It is just like pictures I have seen of early days when people gathered together to celebrate, he said. "May I go and get my wife to come and see?" he asked.

As we shared with Tom and his wife about the meaning of thanksgiving and the plans we had for the next day with the five grains of corn, we had the opportunity to tell Tom how much he had blessed us in the few short weeks since we had moved to the Shrine. Perhaps we need five grains of corn at our plate every day, so each day becomes an opportunity for saying thanks to those who bless us. Don't wait until tomorrow or only once a year to celebrate Thanksgiving Day – do it now, today!

"O taste and see that the Lord is good; And His loving kindness endures forever, even to all generations." Psalm 34:8

Ermine Entertainment

As mentioned in the previous tale, the table was all set and we were anticipating a wonderful time celebrating Thanksgiving Day together with friends. Bob and I got up early to stuff the turkey and begin to prepare the feast for later in the day; then we left for the combined churches worship service in the valley.

During the week previous to Thanksgiving we had an unwanted visitor decide to take up residence in our cozy cabin – an ermine, resplendent in his beautiful winter coat!

For those of you not familiar with this really beautiful mammal it is a highly skilled predator. It kills by delivering a powerful and accurate bite to the back of the prey's neck. Having this slinky, sly animal *inside* our house did not give me much peace of mind as I imagined this furry creature joining us in bed at night. However even with our door closed, thinking this would keep it out of our room, we discovered this wily weasel could flatten itself and slide underneath the door, in this way it could hide almost anywhere in the house; behind cupboards, the frig or stove and it could even climb into drawers.

The ermine, or short-tailed weasel, is small and has a brown or yellowish brown fur in the late spring, summer and early fall months, but then it slowly grows a soft white coat for winter disguise with only a tiny black tip of the tail left unchanged. They have very short legs with sharp claws on the toes, a long snout, big eyes and a long sleek, slender body about 10" with a long narrow tail about 3" which as already mentioned, has a small black tip. They only weigh about 7 ounces, but eat about 40% of their weight every day so are always on the lookout for a meal. They have long sensor whiskers with which they can smell their prey. They are carnivorous creatures (meat eaters) so we never had much of a problem with rats or mice when they were around. However they also prey on animals bigger than themselves like rabbits and they eat eggs, small birds, fish, insects, and berries.

They are prized by furriers for their beautiful winter pelt, but we were not interested in the fur, we just wanted this ermine back out in the forest where he belonged.

Day after day we tried to catch this creature but nothing seemed to work. We just hoped he would not appear and frighten our guests. However Mr. Ermine must have liked the smell of turkey and decided to join the feast much to *our consternation* and the *amusement of our guests!*

So, how to catch an ermine became the entertainment of the day!

The women sat at the table enjoying chitchat and coffee while the men discussed means and methods to outwit the weasel with the white coat. I wish you could have seen the various traps that were constructed all to no avail. The ermine seemed to be just as interested as were we. He would peek out from behind the cupboard to see what was happening, venture into the room, always staying at a safe distance as he eyed the latest trap, then sniff around and retreat before he was caught.

Finally, the men had the perfect plan – *a slide!*

They took a medium length board and applied spoonfuls of peanut butter at strategic intervals to entice the ermine up the "slide" to the top where his weight would cause him to fall into our laundry basket. Once the slide was ready it was placed over near the cupboard behind which the ermine was hiding.

Silence prevailed as everyone watched and waited.

Finally our "Ermine Entertainment" entered from behind the "curtain" cupboard.

The stage was set!

He was very curious but also very careful, watching with his big black eyes for any movement by the men that might threaten his safety. It was simply hilarious to watch him slowly climb up the board holding on with his sharp claws and reaching with his snout for the peanut butter, then quickly sliding back down to safety. But the peanut butter tasted so good he just had to have some more. So back he went.

Over and over we watched in amazement as he would slip and slide on the peanut butter board each time going higher and higher. Then bravery, or perhaps it was greed, took him all the way to the top of the slide and suddenly, without warning, he fell into the basket. I have never seen men move so fast, slam, bam, the lid was on the basket with the ermine inside.

The show was over and announced a *great success* with loud applause, cheers and peals of laughter from the audience. However Grandma Loney was quite distressed when she realized the ermine was to be put *outside*.

"Oh no, she cried, "it is so cold outside."

"He will be just fine" we assured her, "He has a wonderful winter coat to keep him warm!

More coffee and pie ended a wonderful Thanksgiving Day.

As our guests bundled up for their departure one couple said, "Before we came for dinner we had been talking about what to write in our annual Christmas letter and realized we really had nothing much in the way of adventure to share, now we have a wonderful "Ermine Entertainment" tale to tell.

As we've said before, life by the Lynn was never dull and often the source of great entertainment thanks to God's incorrigible creatures like the ermine!

THE WORK OF PRAYER

Introduction

This country was founded on faith and prayer and in 1945 during WWII many of the citizens were deeply concerned regarding the future. It was out of this concern a little magazine was birthed, Guideposts.

"I Believe in Prayer" by Captain Eddie Rickenbacker, was the first little pamphlet printed. Eddie Rickenbacker was a famous flyer and the former President of *Eastern Airlines*. He was honored as one of the greatest heroes of his time. He was known as a man who showed that "faith really works."

The following excerpts from the pamphlet provide a backdrop for this chapter on one of the main aspects of our lives as Caretakers at the Shrine of St Therese – The Work of Prayer. We too "Believe in Prayer."

"There are a lot of things about the human mind and soul that we don't know much about. We get glimpses of them when in times of danger or suffering we cross over the line of ordinary thought. Perhaps such things as the control of mind over matter and the transmission of thought waves are tied up together, part of something so big we haven't grasped it yet, it's part of us and part of 'Something' that is looking after us. It is one of the things that make me believe in personal protection and life after death. I don't know how to put it into words." Rickenbacker then goes on to share some life experiences he had during his flying years. One time he was in France during the war, "with only one magneto on my Newport biplane functioning, I was attacked by three German Albatross planes. I came out of a dive so fast that the terrific pressure collapsed the right hand upper wing. No matter what I tried, I couldn't come out of that whirl of death. I often wished I could think as fast under normal conditions as I did during that drop. While I fought the controls and tried to get the engine going I saw all the good and bad things I had ever done, and most of them were bad. Then I began to pray. 'O God,' I said, 'help me get out of this.'"

Rickenbacker goes on to say, "This escape and others I have had were not the result of any super-ability or super-knowledge on my part. I wouldn't be alive if I had to depend on that. I realized then, as I headed for France on one wing, that there had to be 'Something Else." He comes to this conclusion; "My experiences and the suffering through which I passed taught me that faith in God is the answer to life."

This man called out to God in prayer; God heard and answered!

The following vignettes are times when we called out to God in prayer on behalf of others.

Are You a Father?

In recent years some of the landscape of the Shrine of St Therese has changed, but during our tenure at the retreat center there was a lovely area of green lawn with a picnic table right in front of the main lodge, it was a favourite place for families to gather because right at the edge of the grassy spot was also a wonderful sandy beach area.

As caretakers, one of the things on our daily "to do" list was making sure the atmosphere of the retreat centre was respected. So, when we had retreats in session at the lodge, we sometimes had to ask families to either move to one of the other beach areas further away from the lodge or to keep the noise level down a bit. For the most part people were more than willing to oblige but once in a while they would express their disappointment at the "quiet" rule, pack up their things and leave. I was always sorry when this happened as it was never the intent to spoil family fun.

We also had *lots* of people who came down to just sit in their cars and enjoy the beauty and serenity of the place, but some of them sometimes forgot they had their car radio or tape players set on "loud." It only took a polite reminder and pointing to a sign that asked visitors to respect the "quiet" of the place and they would quickly apologize and turn down the music.

One day a young man drove down the access road in his truck and parked at the edge of the parking lot overlooking the beach. His truck window was down and the noise was so loud we could hear it blaring from *inside* our cabin even with all our windows and doors closed. So Bob went out to ask if he would please turn the music down.

The young man responded by asking Bob a question; "Are you a father?"

"Yes I am, I have four children three of whom are married," Bob replied.

"No, no," the young man remonstrated, "Are you a *Father*, can you *listen* to me?"

Then Bob realized what this man was asking was to talk with a priest.

It seemed logical to assume Bob might be such a person, as after all, we were caretakers at a *Catholic* retreat centre. Bob explained that he was *not a priest* but he was an elder in our own church and would be happy to "*listen*" if the young man wanted to share his problem and then perhaps they could pray together.

A heartbreaking story emerged and the young man told Bob he had come down to the waters edge with suicide on his mind. He said, "The loud noise helps me not think about things." They quietly talked together for some time and finally Bob told him he could stay as long as he needed and if the music helped him that was okay too.

However, it seemed that just being able to talk with someone was sufficient.

The young man smiled and said, "I already feel much better, thank you for listening, I no longer need the 'noise'."

I have a card that says on the front, "Two ears. No waiting!" Sometimes that's all it takes, someone available to listen to a troubled heart and mind.

Are you a *Father?* Can you *listen?* Are you available?

Praise God we have a heavenly Father who is always available to listen and knows exactly how to turn down the "noise" and bring healing to a troubled heart and mind.

Praying For an Eagle

As you know the eagle is our country's national emblem and a most majestic bird; but perhaps there are some facts you might find interesting in regard to the bald eagle.

- On 28th June, 2007 this amazing bird was taken off the endangered species list
- The bald eagle is a member of the sea and fish eagle group
- Bald eagles can fly to an altitude of 10,000 feet and during flight they can achieve speeds of 30-35 mph.
- Bald eagles weigh anywhere from ten to fourteen pounds (I actually thought they might weigh more than this)
- Eagle bones are light because they are hollow
- Wild bald eagles may live as long as thirty years
- The bald eagle is a strong swimmer, but if the water is very cold it may be overcome by hypothermia
- Once their talons are locked round a fish or other catch they are unable to release their hold until they land
- Their diet consists of mainly fish however they will eat carrion (dead and decaying flesh)
- Bald eagles have 7,000 feathers
- They can lift about four pounds in weight
- Bald eagles sit at the top of the food chain
- All eagles are renowned for their excellent eyesight
- Nests are built in large trees near rivers, lakes or by sea coasts
- They lay from one to three eggs
- The thirty five days of incubation duties are shared by both the male and female bald eagle
- The nesting cycle is about 20 weeks
- Today there are about 9,789 breeding pairs of bald eagles
- Once paired bald eagles remain together until one dies

- The bald eagle became the national emblem in 1782 when the Great Seal of the United States was adopted
- It is the symbol on my passport and yours if you have one. Take a look!

We can also learn about eagles from God's Word.

In Isaiah 40:31 we are told, "They that wait on the Lord shall renew their strength they shall mount up on wings as eagles" and in Deuteronomy 32:11 in the Song of Moses we are encouraged with how the Lord provides a shield of protection "like an eagle that stirs up its nest and hovers over its young, that spreads its wings to catch them and carries them on its pinions."

What an amazing picture of how the Lord cares for His people.

Have you ever spent time watching eagles?

As caretakers at the Shrine of St Therese we had many opportunities to do just that because we had eagle nests on the property and daily could observe their lives.

There is nothing more fascinating than to watch an eagle teach an eaglet how to fly. They truly do "spread their wings to catch them" as time after time we observed a young eagle trying to fly and then watched in horror as it began to plummet to the ground. At almost the last minute, or so it seemed to us, the parent eagle would swoop down with incredible speed and spread its wings under the young eaglet and give it what was needed to again begin to soar and try again. Over and over the process was repeated until suddenly on the wings of the wind it took off on its own and we watched in awe as another majestic bird had learned how to fly!

But sometimes watching eagles can be heartbreaking.

One Sunday morning we were getting into our car to head out for our church service in the valley when we noticed an eagle in trouble. His eagle eyes had spotted a fish and he swooped down to catch his breakfast. He was successful with the catch, but had not reckoned on the size of the fish – as his talons locked in place around his prey he found he was unable to take off into the air and head back to his nest.

Now it might seem strange to you, but we just knew we must stay and pray for this eagle, for his ability to make it to shore and for his safety.

Already crows and other birds were flocking around to harass him. We thought he was going to drown before he reached the safety of the shore and could unlock his talons and release the fish. I have never seen such amazing perseverance as this incredible bird using his wings as oars in the water. We sat in our car and prayed for his strength as his wings flapped in the water and inch by agonizing inch he moved himself toward the beach. All the way the crows were dive bombing him and cawing mercilessly at him as though to say, "You'll never make it, just give up we're going to get the fish anyway."

Exhausted, the poor bird finally reached the rocky shore and the instant he let go of the fish the crows were upon it. It was a sad sight to see but we were so relieved he was safe. Now he had to just sit on the rocks until his feathers dried and then try again for another fish breakfast.

Dear friends; God wants us to soar like eagles, but He also wants us to know that when times are tough He is there to catch us, to protect us and to provide for us. If we wait on the Lord He will dry our wings and send us on our way restored and refreshed ready to once again fly on the wings of the wind of the Holy Spirit.

A Father's Ashes

One monthly report notes the following activity:

August, 1995 was a busy month; there were only two days that buildings were not in use. We had quite a few weddings as well as a 25th wedding anniversary. Some of our visitors have had a little more excitement than they expected; a black bear was seen on Shrine Island; the first since we have been here as far as we know.

We have also had our own excitement. Word appears to be out and the Hermitage cabin has become quite popular as a place to spend a night; six reservations this month. After one of the Hermitage occupants left we had a rather anxious phone call the following day. "I wonder if you happened to find a small box in the cabin when you were cleaning up?" his voice betrayed his anxious concern.

When he told us his tale we could understand why!

"I came out to spend the night after my Dad died. He was cremated and his request was to have his ashes scattered around the grounds of the Shrine of St Therese. This I did but there were still some ashes left and I somehow forgot them when I packed up yesterday afternoon."

Bob had already cleaned the cabin and come across the wee box mentioned. At first, not knowing what it was, he was just going to throw it in the garbage, but then for some unknown reason decided to keep it. Praise the Lord, the ashes and the wee box were safe and sound. The young man came the following day and another "first" was noted in life by the Lynn as we returned a father's ashes.

This incident prompted a memory from my childhood. Actually I am not entirely clear as to whether it was *our* family or a story told by my parents regarding *someone else*, as my brother pointed out, these stories are referred to as "Urban Myths" and you can go on line and find a variety of versions; but none-the-less, an ashes story was resurrected from my youth.

During WWII we lived in the Shetland Isles and times were tough. Everyone had ration books to be used when we went to get groceries as many goods were in short supply. We had some good friends living in Australia who quite frequently would send us a variety of cherished goods to supplement our rations. At Christmas time they sent all the ingredients for our plum pudding. Each small packet was carefully labeled so we would know how it should be used. This one year the parcel contained a small packet un-labeled and thinking it just an oversight and that it was some kind of special spice, into the plum pudding it went.

The Christmas treat was all ready for our celebration when a letter arrived. "We hope you got the parcel safely? We also enclosed a small packet of our Uncle's ashes as he wanted to be buried in Scotland; we hope you will do that for us please."

I am sure the pudding was given an appropriate burial in the garden.

I am not sure what we prayed that day – most likely a prayer of thanksgiving that we did *not* eat plum pudding that Christmas.

Another Dead Cat

Bob and I have always taken seriously the work of prayer. This job was no different. So as we worked in the gardens, did repairs to buildings, cleaned and prepared for each group, met with visitors etc we prayed for the Lord to use the time at the retreat centre in each person's life. Often the people who visited were non-believers and many of the retreats were of a secular nature. We often spent time praying during retreats for the leaders and participants. Once in a while a retreat individual or tourist/visitor would ask us to pray for them and this we were most happy to do. Sometimes they came knocking on our door and just needed to talk. Most of the time we never knew if our prayers were answered so it was always encouraging and uplifting when we received good news reports.

One day we had a group from the Juneau Correctional facility; they had come to gather seaweed. The leader of the group stopped to chat and we discovered our paths had crossed before. Back in the 1970's, when he and his family lived in Angoon, they came to Juneau for treatment for a daughter who had cancer; they needed housing and we had room. After they returned to their village we somehow lost contact, but for some time continued in prayer for the daughter to be healed. Now, all these years later, we learned that his daughter was cancer free and doing well.

Sometimes the prayers take years to be answered and others are on the spot.

Early in September one year, a woman "found herself driving down the road to the retreat centre" she said. She told me she had spent hours driving up and down the highway with a dead cat in the car beside her. Distraught and in tears she asked if she could bury the cat somewhere on the grounds at the Shrine. I showed her a place back in the woods and asked if she would like some help, which she refused. So

I returned to our cabin and began praying for her. A half hour later I saw her walking down the road with her shovel, still crying. She just looked so alone and lost, I went out and offered to spend some time with her. We sat in her car and I simply waited for her to speak. Slowly and hesitantly at first she shared about her cat, then suddenly, like a dam breaking, pent up emotions of many other concerns poured out. For an hour or more I just listened and then gently asked if we might pray together; she agreed. She looked at me and smiled, "I feel so much better, thank you for listening; may I give you a hug?"

People come for many reasons and some just "find themselves here" without really knowing why or how; but I believe they are God directed.

Prayer is not always a scheduled activity, for us it is more a life-style, like the air we breathe it fills us up and flows. We know the Shrine of St Therese is a place of refuge and solace for many; churched and un-churched alike; some have left the church and come seeking, others have never set foot inside a church and discover this is a place where they can meet their maker. So we praise the Lord and pray, and thank Him for the many ways He provides for His children.

THE GAP

The Gap

Standing by the side of the road down to the Shrine of St Therese was a tiny log structure; it fascinated me, and I often wondered as I walked past what stories it could tell could the logs speak. It had been built back in the 1930's as a room for individuals to spend some time alone, a very simple place to stay; no electricity, no plumbing, no fireplace...just a room.

As the years passed and it stood unused and almost forgotten the weather began to take its toll. The rafters and roof shakes had already deteriorated and now in 1994 the logs were beginning to rot as well; yet still I could not shake the sense that God had something special in mind for this wee building.

So I began to pray.

I was reading a book one day *"Love on its Knees", by Dick Eastman,* and his message was that we can make a difference by praying for others; "we can *stand in the gap* for others through our intercessory prayers" he said, and suddenly I knew; this dilapidated, falling down building had a purpose. Dick Eastman used Ezekiel 22:30 as his scripture reference for this work of prayer. "I looked for a man among them who would build up the wall and stand before me *in the gap* on behalf of the land so I would not have to destroy it, but I found none." As I read this verse I could feel God's pain because He found *no one standing in the gap.* No one was praying for the land!

A vision began to form in my mind of this cabin restored and moved to a place on the grounds where people of all backgrounds and beliefs could come and spend time in quiet reflection and prayer. It could be a place where individuals could pause and pray for healing, changed hearts, renewal, reconciliation or whatever need the Lord might put on their hearts. And so it was "The Gap" was born.

The Shrine committee agreed to the idea of moving the cabin, and in the fall of 1995 Andrew Vanderjack asked permission to make moving the log cabin structure his Eagle Scout project. **Plan A** was to move it some place nearby in the woods where it could be rebuilt. However after dismantling it and seeing the dry rotted condition of many of the logs, **Plan B** was initiated. This called for some new logs to be selected from a pile of yellow cedar logs and sized to fit in with the usable old ones. And so the task was started. It proved to be a bigger task than first envisioned but Andrew received credit for the portion of the plan that he and Troop #6 accomplished, and in 1997 Andrew received his Eagle Scout award.

Nick Polasky was the next Scout to pursue work on "The Gap" as his Eagle Scout project. He and his crew, also from Troop #6, moved the logs to the designated site overlooking the water; next there was work to be done on the ground to make it level before construction could begin, then came notching the logs to make them fit, a challenging task for these young Boy Scouts. There were openings to cut for a door and also a small window...*many* hours of labour before Nick's portion of the project was completed. In 1997 Nick received his Eagle Scout award for a job well done.

With four, open to the weather, unchinked log walls and no roof "The Gap" sat unfinished for two years. But it was not forgotten! Ben Muse, the third Boy Scout desiring an Eagle Scout project, came on the scene. He and his crew fashioned smaller logs for completing the higher triangular gable walls, the ridge and roof poles were cut and put in place, followed by plywood roofing and finally metal roofing completed the outside structure. Now for the first time a dilapidated log cabin was beginning to look like it might become a place of prayer as one more Boy Scout, Ben Muse, received his Eagle Award in the spring of 2000.

But it was to take two more Boy Scouts along with their crews to fulfill the vision of "The Gap." Chris Barte and Troop 11 volunteers completed the window and with over 1,000 pounds of mortar did an excellent job of chinking between the logs, a task that took great patience and perseverance. But the hard work paid off when in 2002 he also was recognized as an Eagle Scout.

The last Boy Scout, Travis Larsen, also from Troop 11, along with his Scouting buddies, put in many hours of hard work to finish the inside. They mined the recycled asphalt from a storage pile at the Shrine and carried the heavy material through the woods to the cabin site. This was used to provide, a hopefully long lasting, interior floor pad.

Next they hand fashioned an outside door to compliment this amazing log structure. Travis and his crew also hand made some signs to identify and direct visitors to "The Gap." The final touch was preparing the path. These eager beavers dug, pick axed and defined steps to the cabin. Each step was outlined with perimeter logs and gravel was brought in to make the path easier to navigate. In 2002, Travis was the last in line to be awarded for his work on "The Gap" and recognized as an Eagle Scout.

"The Gap" is an answer to prayer; and for me, a dream come true!

It took over seven years but it truly is a place where you can come and intercede, where you can *"stand in the gap"* and as you look out the window, through the woods to the sea and sky and snow capped mountains; the world beyond the confines of this sacred place is brought to the foot of the cross as you spend time on your knees in prayer.

THE WORLD AT OUR DOOR

"On the Job"

A Cross Street

From May through September cruise ships sail the Inside Passage bringing visitors from all over the world. Elegant five and six storied sea-worthy wonders can be seen daily in the Juneau harbour. Some days as many as five ships unload passengers for a day of enjoying the amazing grandeur of glaciers, whale watching, salmon spawning, tram rides, shopping and tours out the road to our retreat centre.

But we also have people coming from all over the world on the Alaska Marine Highway ferry system. Many of these tourists have their own cars and campers and come for more than a day, they want to take time for hiking, canoeing and camping. Many of them have all the latest in technology and are prepared for all kinds of weather. They are very used to finding their way around big cities and know how to get back on track if they make a wrong turn and get lost.

It was the height of the tourist season and we were enjoying greeting and meeting such adventurers. One day we had a phone call early in the morning. "We have just arrived at the Auke Bay ferry terminal and would like to come out to the Shrine of St Therese; we have our own car and just need some directions on how to get there, could you help us?"

That was easy! "Just drive out of the ferry terminal parking lot and turn left on the highway, this is Glacier Highway. Keep driving along this highway until you come to mile twenty-two. You will see a sign on your left at the entrance road that says, "Shrine of St Therese" turn left off the highway at this sign, down a dirt road to the beachside parking lot at the foot of the hill, and you have arrived at the Shrine of St Therese. You can't get lost. It will take you approximately thirty minutes or less depending on how fast you drive and how many times you stop to enjoy the scenery along the way. Please do come and knock on the door at the

Caretakers Cabin to the left of the driveway as you come down we would love to meet you."

"Thank you very much, but can you tell us the name of the cross street?"

"There is no cross street, just the main highway to mile twenty-two and turn left..." "No, no, you don't understand, *a cross street*..." he interrupted and began explaining a cross street. "Yes, I know what a cross street is, but there *is no cross street*, you just turn left..." but before I could finish my sentence he had hung up.

Even a G.P.S. might not have helped this man –
He needed a *cross street!*

Potted Plastic Palm Trees

Every May, we had school children with their teachers who came on Sea Week outings to discover beach treasures found at low tide. Hermit crabs, sea urchins, tide pools full of fascinating wee creatures, squishy seaweed, shells...kids came rain or shine, it made no difference to Alaskan kids, it was a day out of the classroom and an opportunity to roam the beach and have a picnic lunch.

Others came to walk the trails nearby or fish off the rocky promontory of Shrine Island. This area of Lynn Canal is known as "The Bread Basket". Many fisher-folk ply the waters during the summer time catching salmon and halibut, and enjoying the whales, porpoise, and sea lion sightings.

During salmon spawning time the stream bank to the left of the Caretakers cabin was always busy with camera toting curiosity, as visitors watched the annual fish run of salmon trying to get back upstream to lay their eggs and hatch a new batch of salmon. Some of the visitors, not understanding the process would try and "help" the salmon by picking them up and carrying them upstream, so it became a "teaching time" for us as we explained the salmon spawning process and that in every state it is actually illegal to disturb spawning fish. "No Fishing" signs had to be posted but were completely ignored by bears, crows and eagles who enjoyed a feast of rotting salmon flesh. One of the most remarkable things about salmon is how they manage to return to the stream where they were born after migrating thousands of miles from their birth river.

Around the city and borough of Juneau there are a number of camping areas which are set up with camper hook up sites as well as tent camping areas, many of them in very scenic spots near the Mendenhall Glacier or beside the Lynn Canal, however the Shrine of St Therese was not set up for overnight camping and "No Camping" signs were posted during the summer months.

The Shrine of St Therese is situated in a beautiful wooded area of primarily evergreens, mountain ash and alders; so, for visitors in a camper vehicle that drove down the hill and parked by the water's edge, it seemed like the perfect spot to spend the night

They seemed totally oblivious to the sign announcing **"No Camping"** right in front of their parked vehicle and proceeded to set up camp. At first we thought they might be just planning a cookout dinner and then leave. But not only did they have chairs, table, grill and all the makings for a meal, we watched in amazement as they brought forth *green indoor outdoor type carpet and potted trees!* It was already getting late in the evening and most of the visitors had left as we sat inside pondering what to do. We finally decided we needed to check and see if they were indeed planning on camping over night.

"Oh yes," was their enthusiastic reply. "It is such a beautiful place." When we pointed to the "No Camping" sign they were none too pleased. We offered to phone the Director and see if he would give permission for them to stay but they were not interested and simply loudly complained about how selfish we were keeping the beautiful place all for ourselves. They did not seem to hear our repeated offer as they gathered up their gear and stowed everything away. They rolled up the plastic green grass stuffed it behind a seat and with loud complaints drove off up the hill and out of sight. We were left to ponder why anyone would go camping with *potted, plastic, palm trees and green grass!*

Neighbours

The Shrine of St Therese is twenty three miles out of Juneau on the Glacier Highway, and when folks would ask where we lived we'd say, "Out the road."

The City and Borough of Juneau is really divided into four main areas; Downtown, Douglas Island, Mendenhall Valley and Out-the-road. There is really only *one* main highway, Glacier Highway, that extends from the downtown area all the way "out the road" to Berner's Bay where the road ends.

"Out the Road" is the least populated area of Juneau and the further "out" you go the fewer houses you will find, so neighbours are a precious commodity.

There were about four homes nearby but really only one of our neighbours came by to visit us on a fairly regular basis, especially during the summer months. Bernie and his wife Barbara are *long-time* Juneauites and a most delightful couple; but it was Bernie who would wander down the road with his well behaved red Irish Setter and come knocking on our door. We knew if we had time to invite him in we were in for a special treat – he was a veteran story-teller. I wish we had taped his visits because he told such marvelous tales of days long gone.

Bernie loved to tell adventure stories, stories of his days in the armed forces during World War II, stories about animals and life in general. He also loved to tell jokes. We spent many happy hours laughing and chatting over a cup of tea.

Bernie told us he was born in Washington and moved to Juneau in 1935 to work at the AJ mine, but he also shared that he had been the Juneau Chief of Police. According to an article in the *Southeast Alaska Empire, 24th October, 1978* "Hulk was a Juneau policeman for 10 years, from 1945-1955. For nine of those years he was the Chief." When thinking about those years the article relates "He leaned back in his rocking chair with his hands behind his head and said, "Yeah-h-h-h those were the good old days...we didn't have any radios. Whenever we had a call...they'd call a telephone operator, the telephone operator would activate a green light placed around town to signal policemen they were needed." The article shares some of the frustrations the Chief had dealing with prostitution in Juneau, but also the joy of working with young people, the main reason he liked police work he said.

"His eyes crinkle and he laughs when he thinks about some of the unusual occurrences during his stint as Chief. 'We didn't have a jail for a year," he said chuckling. 'Can you believe it? We got by alright. When someone was picked up for being drunk they were driven around in the police car until they were sober again.'"

Bernie was a good neighbour and always available to help if needed. He would faithfully check the place if we were gone and bring the garbage cans down every Thursday from the highway. He would say with a cheeky grin, "This is my tithe to the Catholic church."

But the story that still makes us laugh happened one beautiful summer's day.

Some tourists were visiting and asked us, "Where is the best spot to get some good pictures of eagles?" We offered to ring our good neighbour, Bernie, as he could call the eagles and they would come and perch on his arm and he would feed them, this way they could get some really close up shots. They looked at each other and laughed. Then one of them said, "Sure, why not?"

So we rang Bernie and he invited us up to a pull out spot just beyond the Shrine driveway. I think the visitors were more curious than believing at this point as they followed us in their car to meet Bernie.

After introductions were made Bernie said, "Get your camera all set up and then I will call the eagle to come."

"Yeah... well thanks, it was nice meeting you, but we need to get going," they smiled, in obvious disbelief, as they turned and began walking back to their parked car. Right at that moment Bernie called the eagle and almost instantly a huge, majestic, bald headed eagle descended from the tree tops to land with amazing grace on Bernie's glove covered arm. I called out to the visitors as they were getting into their car, they simply stood with their mouths open in astonishment, but by the time they scrambled to get cameras in place Bernie and the eagle were gone.

It would have been an incredible picture! It makes me wonder; how often does unbelief get in our way and we miss incredible blessings?

About 15-20 years ago Bernie and Barbara sold their house out the road and moved into town, I recall him talking about how sad it was that no one wanted his incredible library of National Geographic magazines; another missed blessing.

A Dinkum Dunnie - Dimes and Drinks

"What on earth is a *dinkum dunnie?*" A dunnie is an Australian term for a toilet, and the word dinkum is another Aussie term which simply means "it's for real." An old Australian song says it well, "I love you fair dinkum, dinky di I do" or in plain English "I really do love you!"

There is a marvellous wee book entitled "Dinkum Dunnies" by Barbara Mullins with fantastic photographs taken by Douglass Baglin of dunnies from all over Australia. I have travelled to many parts of the world and think it would be fun to gather a collection of "dunnies" from all over the world. I have a great picture of a two seater dunnie, side by side toilets, without a door, taken in bush Alaska. I have another one from way out bush in Mongolia with an incredible view across the desert. So when we moved to the Shrine of St Therese we were familiar with outhouses.

There were two outhouses available for visitors labeled Women's and Men's on the rustic wooden doors. The set up was very simple, just a hole in the ground with a wooden seat over it, toilet paper and a can for cigarette butts. Keeping the toilet paper from squirrels in need of soft nesting material was always a challenge. In the summertime we tried to keep them sweet smelling with air-freshener hanging from a nail. However if you visit the Shrine today they have very modern facilities available, handicap accessible and no worries of squirrels getting the toilet paper.

Another thing that has changed with time is the telephone booth.

When we were the Caretakers there was a public telephone box across the road from our cabin which was not only handy for visitors and tourists but also for those who lived out the road and had no access to a telephone. It didn't always work and we quite frequently had to have a repair man come and fix it, in fact we became good friends and he would sometimes stop by for a cup of coffee if he was out the road.

In those days a phone call cost a dime and we very quickly discovered the value of having a wee container full of dimes right by our front door. Can you imagine; a dime for a local call was all that was needed! It would have been interesting to have kept track how many people came by and asked, "Would you happen to have a dime, I need to make a phone call?" I remember a few years later coming home from a trip abroad and discovered a dime didn't work anymore, it was a quarter! Nowadays...Well grandkids have probably never seen a phone booth. "What's a phone booth?" they might ask, in these days of cells phones and I-phones, texting and who knows what's next!

As I think about tourists today and people in general, water has also had an impact on consumerism. Not only can people not live without cell phones but they carry every kind of container imaginable for water – not just plain water either, there are so many varieties of water on the super-market shelves I sometimes wonder how people decide which to buy. Our first summer as Caretakers we realized that only people who rented the Lodge and cabins had access to potable water, as not only were people coming to our door in need of dimes but also wanting a drink of water. We quickly decided it would be simpler to have some paper cups and a large container of water available near the parking lot. So we fashioned a sign, set up the water container with a trash can for the empty cups and one more need was met. Those were the days of dimes, drinks and dinkum dunnies that have somewhat sadly been replaced with all the modern conveniences of society.

THE WONDER AND THE WEATHER

The Wonder of the Weather

Creation

Back in February, 1994, I was sitting in the living room of our log cabin home looking out the window, and was struck by the wonder and glory of God's creation as I watched the waves come crashing in on the beach nearby. I picked up my journal and wrote these words: "As a wave nears the shore it explodes in one accumulated burst of energy; then spent, it spreads itself on rock and sand until nothing is left but foam - but no, not so! Yes it is true it leaves its mark of where it's been, but turning, it recedes to join the depths of other waves, and gaining strength deep cries to deep until once again with strength restored it flows full force with goal in sight and breaks itself once more on sand and shore. With mesmerizing repetition, again and again, all day long the waves replay their age old pattern of life since time began."

Awesome energy
Exploding beauty
Pulsating power
White-capped wonder
Endless flowing
The sea –
It calls to me – come!

So I did.

Out to the glory of a white-capped day I went.
I stopped my journaling
Put on my coat and boots
My wolf-skin fur hat
My warm Shetland wool mittens
And with camera in hand I stepped off the porch into the snow.

The wind had died down and the sun was warm on my
face –

What a day!

The snow spilled over the top of my winter wellies as
I crossed the parking lot and finally made it to the pathway
and across the causeway. The sound of waves crashing on
the rocks filled the cold air and the sun made the snow and
water dance with life as the wind suddenly picked up both
and tossed them in the air. I wanted to yell "hello" to the
whole wide world and hug the sea and sky. I felt I could fly
to the top of the snowcapped mountains across the water and
longed to ride the waves to shore.

It was the kind of day I wished would last forever.

It was a day to lock in the jewel box of my heart to take
out and enjoy again and again; reliving the glory of God's
creation when life needed a lift.

Springtime

Spring and autumn are my two favourite seasons of the year, mostly because I love the brilliant colours of both.

Spring in Juneau is a time when yellow seems to dominate the landscape with skunk cabbage in the ditches and woods, and dandelions begin to take over the lawns and roadsides. We also began to see more sea life as whales migrating from the south arrive for the summer, mink meander up the garden path and squirrels come out of hiding providing signs that spring is on the way.

But for us it was the season of changing chores. Our list of maintenance requirements grew as we investigated building roofs and windows for leaks. As snow disappeared, pipes and other hidden places began to reveal need of repair.

With the snow all gone there was no need for our "Four Wheel Drive Only" sign at the top of the hill and visitors to the Shrine increased considerably. It was time to get the water jug out and "No Camping" signs in place, cigarette butt cans needed to be placed in strategic places along the paths... winter was gone and spring was bursting out all over!

April was traditionally work party month which necessitated a meeting with our boss, Thomas; so early one morning we sat round the kitchen table discussing the "to do" list. Basic spring cleaning was a given so we began making a list of cleaning supplies and equipment to be gathered together. Window washing, dusting and oiling logs walls, pantry shelves organized, defrost the refrigerator, curtains washed, inventory of linen closets and china cupboards etc. Most of this was women's work but there was more than enough for the men to do as well. High on the list was replenishing the firewood supply which had been pretty well depleted over the fall and winter months, picnic tables needed repairing, a sink needed to be reinstalled that had fallen off a wall, painting and gardening; the list seemed endless and we knew it would be impossible to get everything done in *one day*.

However when work party day came around, we had refreshments ready for coffee breaks and all the makings prepared for lunchtime sandwiches, we were always amazed at the work crew that showed up rain or shine. One of the things that impressed us was the dedication and commitment to this retreat facility as people pitched in and worked hard to keep the place running. There was lots of laughter and fellowship as one by one the list of chores was completed. By the end of the day windows sparkled, the wood shed was filled with logs for another year of winter fires and there was a sense of satisfaction from jobs well done.

Spring was also the season of signing! Our work as Caretakers was evaluated as members of the Shrine Board gathered at the Lodge for an evening of fellowship and refreshments. Then Tom Satre, the board chairman, would make some kind remarks and hand us a pen inviting us to commit to another year as Caretakers. Once again we had a decision to make; will we sign on the dotted line? For eight years we never hesitated; we truly *loved our job* no matter the season.

Summer

As I prepared for writing this book I was re-reading some of the reports written for the Board each month and came across this one for July, 1989, it reveals the variety of duties and daily activities involved in Caretaking at the Shrine.

"Things done: Continued lawn mowing, flower bed upkeep, more wood for winter, wiring for electricity in bride's room, gravel on path to outhouses, on-going cleaning and cooking for retreats...With summer sunshine we've had considerably more people using the facilities, picnicking, fishing, bird-watching...almost every day we have small tour busses and taxies bringing visitors as well as camper vans, private cars and motor bikes. We even had a visit from the local police."

In July that year we had our first break in. Someone took a screw driver to the hinge of the money box in the Chapel and broke it open. This was reported to Thomas and the police. We fixed the box and began collecting the money more frequently.

We also had a situation where the local police requested a page from the visitor's guest book as evidence in an accident case.

One of the less enjoyable chores we had to perform during spring, summer and fall seasons was keeping the grounds free of cigarette butts. Especially during the summer this was a never-ending task. We ordered a long handled tool from a catalog which made it a little easier; but we could never quite understand why visitors would frequently just drop their cigarette butts on the ground when a few more steps to a sand filled can would have made our life so much easier.

In summer time we also had more opportunities to take visitors around the grounds and tell them the history of the place. That was fun!

Summer was also the season when we had our own visitors and during our first summers we had family coming home from college for a few months sometimes bringing a friend. In 1989, being our first summer as Caretakers, many friends stopped by to see our "new home." Our family guest book also added names of visitors from Sitka and Texas, as well as Loveland, Colorado when our son, Andrew and his wife, Marilyn came for a week. Our daughter Sharon and husband Bob visited from college in North Carolina and our youngest son David came home from Chicago, Illinois for the summer. So our first summer season kept us on our toes.

From May through August we had an added activity every weekend as local priests, and sometimes the Bishop, provided afternoon mass on Sundays in the Chapel on Shrine Island. Being Presbyterians we had to be instructed in how to prepare the robes and elements for this service. After the Mass the congregation always gathered for a time of fellowship in one of the small cabins, usually the Le Vasseur. So while people attended the service we prepared coffee, tea and cookies; and on cold, wet or rather dreary days we lit a cozy fire.

Water Works

I wonder how many of you have played the game "Waterworks."

It is a game we bought for my husband for his birthday one year when we lived at 15.8 Glacier Highway. He had spent many months working on our plumbing and we sometimes wondered if he should have been a plumber rather than an electrical engineer. The game has many of the tools of the trade and the object is to put spanners and leaky pipes in the path of opponents trying to fix plumbing problems. It is a lot of fun when it is just a game, but sometimes more than frustrating when a real life situation.

Our real life "water works" began in 1993 when the water tank behind the Lodge developed a slow leak. The good rains Juneau and the Valley areas experienced that summer unfortunately did not extend out the road to the Shrine to keep the cistern full. The cistern is higher than the tank and water from the cistern goes to the Lodge first and then back to fill the tank, this of course drains the cistern when the ground water level is low, as it was this particular summer and we had not had any significant rain since early May. The end result was we had to restrict the use of water for cooking and clean up and bare necessities of hygiene which meant retreat participants had to forego showers; even so, the water level kept getting lower and lower in the tank.

The stream to the south of our log cabin also suffered through the drought and kept getting lower and lower until it just petered out at about mean tide level. Fortunately just down from where Father Hubbard's boat, The Libby, was parked there was a spot deep enough to fill a *very small* bucket. So for flushing toilets we filled bigger buckets from the small one and carried them to the Lodge, Post Office Cabin and our house.

There were many bucket brigades, some more cheerful than others, as the water work continued. Finally, with about three feet of water left, Thomas and John Monagle decided to bring in water. A 500 gallon tank was borrowed from Cameron Plumbing and Heating and brought out in John's pick up truck.

It was rather like a scene from "I Love Lucy" as the saga played out.

Bob writes in our report, "I got hoses and extension cords... and held my finger over the hole where the pump pipe broke off when the tank fell off the pickup so all the water wouldn't run down the driveway...then John held his finger over the hole while I ran to get some duct tape and other stuff to plug the hole. Then John and another man ran to get Thomas so they could get another pump. Meanwhile, I made a sign to put at the top of the driveway warning people the driveway was blocked."

At the end of the day there was about five and a half feet of water in the tank but that week we had a group from a "lower 48"church coming for two weeks, so there was still need for bucket brigades for flushing toilets and a sign on bathroom doors announcing "No Showers." They were a great group. One of the men headed out one day and brought back two electric pumps.

Bob tells the next episode this way; "When I tried them out (the pumps) they both worked and the sump pump looked like new. As I was getting tired of hauling water from the creek I decided to make life easier for myself and the people in the Lodge. I installed the sump pump in the creek almost directly under the "some-day bridge" girders where the water level was about a foot. To do this I first drilled holes around the bottom of a bucket to try and keep trash and stuff getting in and put the pump into the bucket. I tied ropes to the pump and put rocks around the bucket to keep the whole thing from falling over. Next I ran a hose and electric cord from the hose to our fenced yard so I could just go out our bedroom door, plug in the electric cord in the outside socket and get water just a few yards from our bathroom. It worked really well. The next day Thomas came out and we added more hose to the system running it to the tank behind the lodge. Now we could fill the tank with water from the creek...or so we thought. However the pump was not strong enough to get the water over the top edge of the tank. "

So another brain storm session!

"I rummaged around in my stuff in the garage and found an old impeller pump. It didn't even go around but I thought it might with a little work. So I took it apart, cleaned it, bent some of the cooling fan blades into place so they wouldn't stop it from going round, messed with the brush holder that was partly rusted away until it finally worked."

By this time Thomas had left for the day. But Bob kept working. He got electricity to the "like new" impeller pump by running an extension cord through the window of our bathroom and connecting the pump into the hose line. It was enough booster power to get creek water into the tank. Hallelujah!

It lasted about a day and night and then "kaput" the wee impeller pump died. But we had about a foot of water added to the tank.

But that was not the end; Bob is not a quitter.

He rummaged around and found another pump; (how many pumps can you gather in a lifetime) one that is put on an electric drill. However this one also needed repairs. After trying three drills he finally found one that went fast enough to have decent water flow; so the system was once again working. It worked for quite a few days except several times vehicles ran over the hose and squashed it, causing leaks.

Duct tape to the rescue!

There were a number of other ingenious inventions to keep the system going, but finally the tank overflowed and the retreatants could relax and enjoy themselves.

The August report that year was eighteen pages in length and the "water works" was only one aspect of our activities.

The following summer, 1994, we were once again dealing with water; however this time it was not so much leaking pipes as trying to fill a new 12,000 gallon water tank.

It took almost six days and five pumps to fill it with water from the creek on the other side of our log cabin and doubled the electric bill in comparison to the previous year at the same time. But we were so very thankful to finally have running water in our pipes again, even if at first it was only good for flushing toilets and washing dishes.

That summer we had only 5-6 days of rain until the first week of September, yet Juneau is well known as *rainforest terrain*. Global Warming! What do you think?

A Second Story Escapade

The exact time of departure of the afore-mentioned Water Works group from out of town, had never been put down in black and white, only that they had to catch an early plane around 6:30-7:30am on Sunday morning. The next group was scheduled to arrive that same morning at 10am and as we usually left around 8am to attend our worship service in Auke Bay they had been advised by Thomas not to expect we would have had time to clean the Lodge, especially as Bob was holding down the fort on his own while I was on a trip.

One of the couples from out of town asked if they could leave their car over night on Saturday and come back early Sunday to pick it up after seeing their friends off at the airport as they were staying in Juneau at some other place for an extra four days of sightseeing before heading back home. No problem, Bob told them, as long as all their belongings were out of the lodge before 10am.

Just before leaving for church Sunday morning Bob went over to the lodge to check and see if lights etc were turned off and the place was at least somewhat picked up for the in-coming retreat. As planned, the door was locked. He had given the group leaders the key to the front door of the lodge on Saturday evening and arranged for them to hide it in an agreed on place for the in-coming group. We had done this in the past and it worked well. He went to the hiding place and the key was not there, however the back door had been left unlocked. The back door gives entrance to the lodge pantry and supply room and has a connecting door into the kitchen. This door can be locked from the kitchen side; which we sometimes did if a group were providing their own meals and did not need access to the pantry. So while Bob had gained access to *the pantry* he was still effectively locked out of *the rest of lodge* because someone had turned the key on the kitchen side of the door *and locked it!*

So off he went to get a ladder and a screw driver. Climbing up the ladder to the south-end second story bathroom window, he managed to pry it open with the screw driver; then climbing over the window sill in his Sunday go-to-meeting suit he finally gained entrance to the building. Now he was able to unlock the door between the kitchen and the pantry, but was still unable to unlock the front door to the lodge without the lost key. He spent a few minutes looking around to see if it might have been left on a table or somewhere on a counter but *no key!*

It was obvious that the couple had not moved out as their things were still in a downstairs bedroom and bathroom and food items in the kitchen, so he assumed they had taken the key with them and hopefully would be back in time to move out before 10am and the key would be in its hiding place for the next group.

Around noon, the Chapel by the Lake service was over and it was time to go back to the Shrine. The Lodge was obviously occupied and the new retreat in full swing; he later learned they had found Bob's note on the front door inviting them to enter via the back door and pantry. About 4pm the couple came back for their car and other personal effects and as Bob was busy on a long distance phone call he did not have an opportunity to talk with them and find out what had happened before they drove off up the hill.

Later that evening Bob checked and found the missing key safe and sound in its wee hiding place. "Another episode for your book," said Thomas as he agreed to the suggestion that it might be good idea to have another key made for future emergencies.

Autumn Change

The end of summer brings change. For one thing; it is time to return to school. At the end of August, 1990 our son David and our summer-son Jim, a friend of David's, had to leave and head back to Moody Bible Institute. They had spent the summer months living with us at the Shrine while working for Tempsco Helicopters, a flight-seeing company that took locals and tourists up over the Juneau ice fields. During that summer along with the usual every day, all year-long activity, we also:

- measured and weighed halibut on our bathroom scales
- mended a motor bike helmet
- provided weather reports for fishermen during the Salmon Derby
- provided wind reports for folk wanting to go wind surfing
- removed a fish-hook from a birds mouth
- housed and fed a dog and finally found the owners... the list goes on and as

Charles Dickens says, "Nature gives to every time and season some beauties of its own and from morning to night, as from the cradle to the grave, is but a succession of changes so gentle and easy that we can hardly mark the progress." And so comes autumn, when the leaves, once green, begin to turn shades of gold, bronze and red. The whales and birds begin their migration south to warmer climes and the humming birds hitch a ride on the backs of Canadian geese.

We were told a story about a humming bird that missed its flight one year and got left behind. Friends found the wee thing shivering in the cold on their deck. So they rang Alaska Airlines to see if they would take the tiny creature on their next flight south. "Sure enough," they said. So, on the wings of an Alaska Airlines morning flight that humming bird had *First Class* service, non-stop to warmer weather in the south. Can you imagine the conversation when that wee bird greeted its friends as they arrived on the backs of the geese and asked, "How did you get here so fast?" "*Alaska Airlines* rescued me. It was simply incredible. Hey, you should try it next year; I think that's the *only* way to fly!"

The advent of fall signals change for Caretakers also. In October we often had big wind storms and trees came down, sometimes landing on power lines or across the access road. Chain saws came in handy and we were grateful for men quick on the scene to restore power and safety.

During the summer-time we had lots of family reunions and camping groups but in the autumn that changed as local government, schools and business groups took a day or over-night retreat to get their group organized for the next nine month season of work; City and Borough Community Development, Department of Family and Youth, Over-eaters Anonymous, R.E.A.C.H, Floyd Dryden School, Northern Sales, Color Me Mom, Capitol City Quilters...to name a few.

One October a Catholic group, "The Lady of the Rosary," was having a retreat led by Sister Judy Gomila and we were invited to join them. Bob was already over at the Lodge but I had decided to have a quiet day at home and was still in my pyjamas sitting by the fire when there was a great commotion at the door; people singing and laughing walked right in and threatened to kidnap me if I did not willingly get dressed and "get on over to the retreat." As I did not relish being dragged out into the cold and windy autumn day in my night attire, I gave no argument and quickly promised to get dressed.

The fall air was full of fun that day and we came home most refreshed!

A Weather Report

If we were giving the weather report for August, 1991 it would be;
- *RAIN!*
- No lawn mowing; *it rained*
- No painting; *it rained*
- The roof of our cabin leaked because; *it rained*
- The month of September was a little wet because *it rained*
- Our daughter, Sharon helped me with the bulletin board in the lodge and decided that an umbrella with *rain-drops* would be appropriate!
- It was a good month, if you like *RAIN!*

And Phone Evangelism

Our life by the Lynn opened up a new and interesting way of reaching people for the Lord; we called it *"Phone Evangelism!"*

People came to use the phone on a regular basis. One was a woman going through a divorce and she needed to use the phone almost every day. Often after she was finished she would accept the invitation for a cup of coffee; she just needed a listening ear.

At one point in time we had what we lovingly called "Our Women's Commune" living out the road. There were four women, all of them very independent, rugged individuals who lived alone and appeared to be very self-sufficient. For some unknown reason they all came to visit us one very stormy evening. We were in the process of clearing away trees that had fallen across our driveway, so they all pitched in and helped then came in for a cup of tea and a cozy chat by the fire. Our phone often proved to be a life line for them when they got lonely or needed help. After phone calls were made they would sometimes stay and visit awhile; and that is when our "phone evangelism" began.

We also met some interesting phone repairmen; our phone seemed to have a lot of problems. The fall of 1991 we had to have the whole system checked and the place re-wired because we began to have music and radio interruptions as well as all our neighbours' conversations crossing ours. One repairman said, "I think you have evil spirits messing up your lines" well, it's possible, especially as our ministry was "phone evangelism." Who knows, but it was a reminder to pray for protection of ministry at the Shrine and a realization that our work as Caretakers was much more than cleaning and maintenance; we rejoiced in the opportunities to share our faith with people the Lord put across our path.

Winter Wonderland

In Juneau, as we come to the end of August and head into September and October, there is always a question on everyone's mind; "When will it come?" When *"it"* comes it is called "termination dust."

Termination dust, or snow as most people call it, signaled the end of autumn and the beginning of winter. For us as Caretakers, it usually brought with it a sense of *urgency* as we worked hard to get everything winterized before temperatures dropped to freezing.

One year however it was a race against time to get the Hermitage Cabin wired for power and fans and outlets fixed for power in the Chapel. After I learned that Bob had tied himself to a tree to get the electrical wiring across the creek to the Hermitage Cabin I was rather anxious when I saw him taking a very tall ladder across the causeway to the Chapel and realized he would be climbing to the top of it to wire the fans in the ceiling.

"Don't worry," he assured me, "I will tie myself to the rafters if necessary." I am not sure that was any great comfort however, as I imagined him swinging from the rafters unable to get his feet on the ladder, or some other equally nightmarish scenario!

As you can imagine instead of mowing lawns we now shovelled snow. Once, when asked what he had been doing for the past couple months, Bob said, "Shovelled snow, shovelled snow and shovelled snow. Then, cleaned the Lodge, cleaned the Lodge, and oh yes, cleaned the Post Office and Le Vasseur cabins and for a change; shovelled snow!"

One winter we were greatly concerned about having enough oil to make it through winter until spring thaw when the oil truck could make it down our hill. The road was extremely icy and we were not sure if the delivery truck would be able to make it *down* the treacherous hill, let alone *back up again!* Even with our four-wheel drive vehicle it was sometimes touch and go. One day I tried to put sand in strategic spots to make it a little easier, but ended up sliding on my behind all the way to the bottom of the hill. It was like a roller coaster ride with no way to stop until I ran into a snow bank.

Bob said, "We better begin praying for an increase in oil." The *very next day* an oil man appeared at our door. He had made it down and filled the tank. Now we prayed he would be able to get back up the driveway without a catastrophe. He did! Praise the Lord for a major miracle!

We had a sign at the top of the hill alerting drivers, "Four-wheel Drive or Chains Only." But unfortunately not everyone paid attention, even the Governor of Alaska and his entourage decided they could make it. He was somewhat chagrined when he had to come and ask Bob for a tow back up to the top of the hill. He insisted on paying Bob $20 for his help.

Some days crossing the causeway to open the Chapel for possible visitors and again to close it at the end of the day was truly an adventure. I can recall only one time however, that we simply could not get across. The wind was so strong, whipping up the waves on one side of the causeway and tossing them clear across to the beach on the other side. With a walking stick for aid I managed to get from the Caretakers Cabin to the edge of the causeway, but every time I tried to walk across the path to the island the wind literally blew me backwards almost knocking me over. But it was exhilarating as I leaned into the wind and it held me. It reminded me of my childhood in Shetland when I would stand at the top of a hill with my girlfriend and we would unbutton our coats, raise them behind us like a sail and then leaning into the wind we allowed ourselves to be lifted up and carried to the bottom of the hill. What an adventure.

In 1993 Bob was gone for almost a week, it seemed like a month to me because wouldn't you know it; we had our biggest snow-fall for that winter that week! Now, I enjoy shovelling snow, but that week it seemed a never ending task, as soon as I got paths cleared it snowed again. I would shovel my way out to open buildings and by the time I had opened doors and done chores I had to shovel my way home again. So I decided to make shovelling snow my ministry and would say to myself, "One shovel load for God, one for others and one for the Shrine...Once in awhile it had to be *two for God* just to keep me going!

In January, 1994 Bob wrote our report "January was a light month as far as use of the facilities was concerned but was more than made up for with snow. It was almost a full-time job removing snow when the Sitka Tribe were here from Sunday to Thursday...it seems like I have been spending 3-6 hours every day for the past week or so using the snow-blower or shovel, and at present I'm snowed in. The snow stopped and the weather warmed up so the snow melted and has become too heavy for the blower to work. Tuesday it took *two hours* to make one path up the driveway. By then I was out of energy and daylight...but at least there was a path to take the garbage up to the highway on Wednesday..."

Another January we had a couple of adventurous women coming to stay at the Hermitage Cabin across the creek, so Bob headed out to take some wood over, light the stove and have the cabin warm and ready when they arrived. Many places the snow had turned to ice and Bob thought the easiest way over the creek was to wheel the barrow across one of the two ice-covered metal girders that had been put in place ready for spring when a bridge would be built. I still cringe when I think about him pushing that barrow full of wood "tight-rope" style across the icy metal girder high above the river.

When Thomas heard about it he said in no uncertain tones, *"No more!"*

The next week Bob had to wheel the barrow *through* the icy creek and *up* the snowy bank…not quite as treacherous but still no picnic. Come spring we decided one of the items on the "to do" list would be; *build a wood shed* beside the Hermitage Cabin!

But none-the-less, we loved wintertime!

Tom Satre came often and ploughed, leaving beautiful piles of snow along the edges of the grounds, icicles hung from roofs and tree limbs covered with pristine white snow took on grandeur and grace that left us speechless. At the ocean edge and all along the rocky shore, snow crystals formed, and when the sun shone they sparkled like a million diamonds. It was also the season to curl up by our wood-burning stove with a cup of cocoa and read a good book.

In autumn we asked, "When will the snow fly?" but in January and February we began to wonder, "When will it thaw?" However, eager as we were for the snow to melt, it ushered in other problems; as the snow melted the parking lot became a lake and, with no outlet from the high, snow-bank boundary and temperatures still dropping to below freezing at night, the lake became a huge skating rink to cross each day to reach the Shrine facilities. I have always wanted to be a skater, but I never learned how. Now, it was learn the hard way, and I had lots of bruises to prove I tried. For me it was mostly slip and slide! But winter eventually gives way to spring and once again we discovered; as an unknown writer once said, "We are not deserted by an unfeeling Creator to the crippling brutalities of wind, snowdrifts, sleet and ice. Spring is on the way. Every snow and ice covered bud witnesses to that prophetic hope!"

CROW ISLAND

The Chapel

Shrine Island was originally called Crow Island because of the abundance of crows nesting in the trees, the name may have changed but it is still a favourite site for crows today.

According to material Thomas Fitterer has provided, in the summer of 1937 (the year I was born) George Murphy, a volunteer from New York, arrived on the scene.

"George cleared off the trees, grubbed out the stumps, dug the trenches for the concrete foundation, and helped pour the concrete footings in preparation for the stone structure that was to be the focus of construction the next year." He did all this hard work "free of charge and without any previous experience in this line of work." He returned in 1938 to assist with the construction of the chapel.

Next in line was a man named D.P. "Doc" Holden. He was a stone mason by trade but also took on the role as foreman of the building project. Originally the Shrine Chapel was to be a log structure but; "due to a severe storm, most of the logs that had been cut were scattered and washed out to sea." But in this too we see the hand of God at work; Doc was a stone mason and there were plenty of rocks available, so a change of plans and work moved forward.

Doc was also responsible for the building of the massive stone fireplace in the Lodge. He and his wife lived in one of the wee cabins at the site while he supervised the work. Doc is quoted as saying, "We had a hundred dollar truck, wheelbarrow, a mortar box, mortar hoe, rope and fall for hoisting stone, and a handmade skip. There were some bad times, but the work continued, and in time the chapel structure was completed."

There is a saying that proved true, "Many hands make light work"

Rocks were gathered from the shores around the island and beaches nearby by willing workers, many of them school children from St Ann's Catholic School in Juneau, also Boy Scouts as well as unemployed men needing work who were rewarded with a meal for their hard work.

"On 30th October, 1938, the Feast of the King, many gathered on Shrine Island for the laying of the cornerstone in the outside bell tower wall. Bishop Joseph Raphael Crimont S.J., bishop of all the Territory of Alaska, blessed the corners which held a copper box containing time capsule items, written information, newspapers and a film of the blessing ceremony. In October, 1988 both Bob and I were present for the opening of this box and the 50th anniversary Liturgy celebration with Bishop Michael Kenny officiating. We were even given the privilege of placing something in the box; now hidden away in the rock wall until October, 2038.

Another skilled man involved with this building was Harry Ellingen. He built the pews, still in use today, out of Southeast Alaskan yellow cedar and also the hardware for the massive wood doors.

There have been many changes over the years; for one thing it now has electricity and with a new roof and windows it is a much more energy efficient building. Also in October, 2002 a ramp was constructed, making it handicap accessible.

As Thomas noted; "The Shrine Chapel has been a very spiritual center for local Juneau people and thousands of travelers and pilgrims over the last sixty plus years...The Shrine was built on a foundation of love and this foundation remains today."

Shrine of St Therese Chapel
Photo by Jon and Phoebe Sandstedt

Stations of the Cross

One of the most beautiful walks visitors to Shrine Island can take is around the perimeter of the island on a winding trail through the woods. All along the way are stopping places at the Stations of the Cross. "Each sheltered face is 24'x18' and the original scene placed in it was a picture protected by a glass covering. The damp climate penetrated these and in 1966 cast stone figures were set in place."

For many years there were only fourteen stations, until a man named R.D Robinson agreed to create new sculptures for each of the fourteen stations and also a fifteenth station honouring the Resurrection of Christ. Each of these new creations is cast from alabaster and onyx and the faces are described by Robinson as "a contemporary Renaissance style." Over the months as he visited the Shrine to work on this project we got to know this very special man and always enjoyed a chat.

The fifteenth station is my most favourite. All of the others are *inside* a wooden railing that goes around the rocky promontory, a very necessary protection as the cliffs dropping down to the rocky beach and ocean below are steep and dangerous. But the fifteenth station is built into a rocky outcropping *outside* the railing, with the stunning backdrop of ocean and Chilkat Mountains, it is most inspiring. To me, it seemed most fitting that R.D. had placed the cross *outside* the confines of the island fences; Jesus was crucified *outside* the city. He lived a life that was *outside* of what so many on the *inside of society* wanted. He calls to each of us to come *outside* of our comfort zones.

This Resurrection Cross, standing alone on a rocky outcropping beyond the boundaries of safety, challenged me to move beyond the limits of what I know, to the unknown. The Resurrected Christ knows the way and goes before me calling me to come *outside* and experience Resurrection Life!

At the end of a busy day one of the things I greatly enjoyed doing, was to go out to the island and stand by the rustic wood railing and look out beyond the shore to the distant horizon and watch the sun go down. Often as I stood in the peace and quiet of the evening hour my eyes were drawn to this fifteenth station in the foreground. One evening I took about ten or fifteen pictures of the Cross, the fifteenth station, as the sun began dipping below the horizon, the end result was a glorious sunset with a silhouetted cross in the foreground. Thomas liked it so much he asked if the Shrine could buy copyrights to the picture.

"The Candle Ceremony"

As previously mentioned, one of the things we did as Caretakers twice a day, morning and evening, was walk out across the causeway to Shrine Island to the stone chapel. It was our responsibility to lock or unlock the door. We were the "keepers of the key," a very large metal key to the massive wooden door.

It was something we *really* enjoyed doing.

The building was left open during the day for visitors to enter and have a time of prayer and contemplation as well as read the history of the place or browse through the pages of a wedding album.

Not only did we lock and unlock the massive wooden door with the huge key, we also kept the floor swept, the pews dusted and polished, the heat turned on and off and any other things needing attention. Another daily chore was to light the candles on the altar each morning and be sure they were extinguished in the evening.

On one of our first days in our Caretaking career, a good Catholic friend, Mary Horton, came out with me to open the building. As we walked into the Chapel she went forward to the altar and lit the candles, then she picked up a bell sitting on a table nearby and rang it a couple of times before replacing it back in its place. We were new to the ways of opening and closing the Chapel so I observed all this with great interest.

The next time I went out I followed her example, and every day thereafter for eight years, on opening and closing the Chapel I rang the wee bell a couple of times in what I called, "The Candle Ceremony."

When it became known that we would be moving and no longer be the Caretakers this same friend came out to spend some time with me. At the close of the day she walked over to the Chapel with me and sat quietly in a pew as I did the closing chores finishing with the "Candle Ceremony."

As we walked back over the causeway she asked, "Why did you ring the bell?"

I was quite surprised by her question; "Well, eight years ago when you came out with me I watched very carefully how you lit the candles and then rang the bell a couple of times, so I assumed this was important!" She burst out laughing. "Oh Christie, I just rang the bell for fun, it had no meaning whatsoever. I like the sound of bells."

We both had a good laugh.

Some days later, at the farewell party at the Lodge, Mary came over and handed me a wee package, inside wrapped in tissue paper was a beautiful brass bell with a wooden handle. Inscribed on the side are the words;

"Caretakers; Bob and Christie Loney, October '88 - June '96."

I still have that precious wee bell sitting on the buffet in our dining room. Every time I look at it I chuckle as I recall Mary and my "Candle Ceremony."

Take Off Your Shoes

In October, 1988 Bob wrote the monthly report and noted, among other things, "Of course the Chapel has been unlocked and locked morning and night and the Holy candle lit and extinguished." Then he shared the following experience:

"The first time I went out to close up it was a dark night. We had not moved our flashlights from our other house to the Caretaker's house yet but I had a candle-lantern that showed the path just a few feet in front of me, enough not to stumble on a rock but not much more. I thought as I walked along of *Pilgrim's Progress and Christian* – *"light that showed only enough at a time"*.

When I stepped into the Chapel and closed the door behind me I immediately was compelled to start praying in a spiritual language, (not the first time I have done that by any means). Then the words came, "Take off your shoes for you are on Holy ground!" I immediately obeyed."

This story reveals what many experience not only in the Chapel environment but throughout the grounds of the Shrine of St Therese. It is often referred to as "holy ground." One November day I was walking along the highway above the Shrine and as I came to the turn-out near Bernie Hulks place the Lord seemed to say, "Go across here and look down at the Shrine." From this vantage point you can see the wide expanse of Shrine Island, the causeway and beaches, some of the other buildings, Lynn canal and the Chilkat mountains in the distance.

I crossed the road as directed by the Lord, and as I stood looking at the peaceful scene below, with the sparkling water and snow-capped peaks the questions came,

Why is this place so special?

What makes it different from other places?

What draws people here?

God spoke in my heart, "It is Holy ground because it is *dedicated to me* and people know that."

Then the Lord showed me how Pearl Harbour, situated to the right of Shrine Island, is in the shape of a large "C" and He said, "This stands for 'Consecration' this place is *consecrated* and is to be used for *my* purposes."

During our eight years at the Shrine we had a deep knowing of this God given insight and experienced the truth of those words as we spent time with Thomas and members of the Shrine community.

The Shrine of St Therese is very much a place dedicated and consecrated to the Lord and those who come to use the facilities and enjoy the grounds quickly become aware of the atmosphere and sense that it is indeed Holy ground!

TIME OUT

The Caretakers Take Some "Time Out"

A Night at the Movies

We chose early on in our married life to not have T.V. in our home. In fact when we went to the Lower 48 for vacations and our kids made lists of what they wanted to do, the first two items were usually;

1. Go to McDonalds
2. Watch TV

In those days we did not have a McDonalds in Juneau, and when one opened up, people even came in small planes from the outlying villages of Southeast Alaska and camped in the newly paved parking lot waiting to be first in line for a hamburger, fries and a milkshake. When it finally opened they broke the record for opening sales of any McDonalds anywhere in the U.S.A.

But back to the TV!

When we moved out to the Shrine of St Therese we still did not have TV and the only one available to us was a very small one, about a 12' screen, in the gift shop. At that time, the gift shop was set up in a rather dark, stone floor and walls, cold and somewhat musty, wee room at the back of the Chapel.

It was winter time and we decided to have a night out, but since there had been a very heavy snow fall that day and it was a long way to the valley, we opted for a movie across the causeway in the, somewhat like a dungeon, small room.

So we put on warm coats, hats, gloves, thick socks and winter wellies and armed with blankets and pillows, hot chocolate in a thermos, pop-corn already popped in bags and the movie "Anne of Green Gables" we set out to trudge across the causeway, through the deep snow, for our night at the movies!

Looking back on that evening, it is hard to believe we lasted for the length of the show. It was not exactly comfortable, the stone floor was, well a *stone floor,* and even with pillows and blankets all snuggled up together, you could see our breath in the air. It was extremely *cold!*

I think it was a great adventure, but as our youngest son said, when we came home from a one o'clock in the morning, beach BBQ picnic one New Year's Eve; "It was fun but it is not something we need to make into a *tradition!*"

However, I am sure it was just the kind of adventure "Anne with an e" would have thoroughly enjoyed!

A Dinner Date

There were some months we simply had no time for dates, work at the Shrine, family activities and especially when I was working at the Christian school in the valley as well as the Caretakers job at the Shrine, a 'time out" was somewhere over the rainbow of our dreams.

When Thomas brought the next month's work schedule, Bob and I would sit down with a cup of tea and our calendar to look at the number of days the facilities were booked. We noted how many groups requested meals, and how many retreats were back-to-back with little time in-between for a break, how many weddings, how many buildings were being used at the same time... In the beginning there were times we would think to ourselves, "No way, impossible!"

But as the months passed we began to experience an amazing truth at work in our lives; we discovered the Lord never gives you more than you can handle without providing a way out. During months which initially had almost no days of reprieve from retreat groups on site and all the buildings were in use for days on end, something would miraculously change. Unexpectedly a group would cancel at the last minute, Thomas would appear and offer to clean one of the buildings or someone would drive down to our house with a batch of cookies and say, "I just thought you might like some extra help with meals..." and there would be time to take a deep breath and maybe even a picnic lunch at the beach!

We had just come through a month like the ones described and had another one on the horizon, our son had been home from college for the summer and had just left, I was taking a two-year intensive Bethel Bible Training class every Wednesday evening at our church, which I really enjoyed, but it required a lot of home-work and memorization...it was a very busy time but we were managing okay, or so we thought!

One Friday afternoon we needed to go into the valley to do some grocery shopping for a group arriving that evening, everything was prepared and we had no meals to serve until the next day. So we made our shopping list and took off to enjoy the drive along the Glacier highway to Fred Meyers. Somewhere between produce picking and bakery buying our taste buds woke up and said, "Smells good, let's eat!" so spur of the moment we decided to eat dinner at a restaurant before heading home.

Caretaker chores were *totally* forgotten as we enjoyed a very delicious meal made even more scrumptious by the fact neither of us had to cook. As we sat relaxing over coffee and pie Bob said, "Would you like to go to a movie?" It had been a coon's age since we had been to a *real* movie theatre, sitting on comfortable seats instead of a stone cold floor and with a bucket of *hot* buttered pop-corn.

I don't remember what movie we saw, but it was really late by the time we drove down the hill to home. We noticed lights were on in the lodge, but it simply did not register that a group had arrived and that we had not been there to let them in. We were still in the twilight zone of a world where we had nothing but relaxing and warm fuzzies on our minds. Our wake-up call came the next morning when someone came knocking on our door...How could we have forgotten *everything*? It was a case of *total amnesia!*

Guess we were not doing so well. But, it was a dinner date we will *never forget!*

A Day at the Beach –A Double Blessing

In the fall of 1993 I had an opportunity to go on a mission trip to Taiwan for three weeks. So thanks to my husband's willingness to keep the home fires burning and the Shrine Committee agreeing to step in and help him as needed I took off on an amazing adventure. The team of about eight men and women from many parts of the USA spent most of the time in hands on ministry, prayer and teaching about the work and person of the Holy Spirit.

We flew into the northern city of Taipei where we spent the first few days and then travelled by train down the west coast to Hsinchu, then on to T'aichung before going across the island to Hualin, down the very scenic east coast to Taitung and on to Kaohsiung a city in the southwest of the island nation. All along the way we had meetings in churches and homes so there was very little time for sightseeing and play; it was a teaching trip and while I thoroughly enjoyed what we were doing, at times it was quite exhausting.

By the time we reached the southern city all of us were really ready for a *day off*, but we had an important day of teaching planned before we would board the flight back to the U.S.A. However, Brad Long, our team leader greeted us at breakfast and announced he had arranged for a van to take the team on a daylong trip to a beach. There were jubilant shouts of excited response as everyone hurriedly ate breakfast and headed off to prepare for a day of sightseeing and beach fun.

Now anyone who knows me even slightly knows that one of my favourite things to do is a picnic; and probably the *most favourite* is a *picnic at the beach!* As I sat on the steps of the church waiting for the van to arrive, in my mind, I was already walking along the sandy shore, picking up shells, jumping in and out of the waves and enjoying a picnic lunch with my friends.

It was time to get on board and as I walked toward the van a most familiar *voice* interrupted the picnic plan with, "*You need to stay and pray for Brad!*" It was not a request it was a *command!* I somehow knew there could be no arguing, so I turn to one of the team members and said, "I am sorry, but I really need to stay and pray. Brad will be teaching all day and if we all go to the beach he will have no one in the room covering him with prayer." Yes, I was disappointed, I love the beach so much I could hardly believe I was obedient to the Lord's call, but; in some unexplainable way, there was joy in the decision. My choice was clearly affirmed by everyone because no one tried to dissuade me from the decision, they simply said, "We will miss you. God bless!"

At the last minute another member jumped off the bus and said he really needed to stay because he had important business that couldn't wait, his ticket home the next day was not confirmed. So while he went off to take care of his business I joined Brad in the sanctuary where he had already begun teaching a group of pastors. Brad spoke fluent Chinese and I did not understand a word he was saying or even the topic for the day, so I sat quietly in the back of the room praying.

I had been praying for quite a long time when my silent prayers were interrupted by *a very familiar voice*, "You need to tell Brad, it is time to stop speaking and to give the men time to practice what he has been teaching." I did not feel the least bit comfortable interrupting Brad, but *The Voice* was insistent, "NOW!"

So rather hesitantly I interrupted the teaching, "Brad, excuse me please, but the Lord has just spoken to me as I was praying and I think you are to stop speaking and give the pastors time to practice what you have been teaching." Brad listened to what I said and without making any reply turned to the pastors and spoke in Chinese. Suddenly they all burst out laughing. I sat feeling very uncomfortable, wondering what was so funny. Then Brad turned and smiled at me, "I just told the pastors what you said, we are all laughing, because I had just finished saying to them in Chinese that we should take a break and practice what I have been teaching, then you interrupted and said the exact same thing in English. I have spent the morning teaching them about how to hear God's voice and how to know it is Him speaking. Your interruption is amazing confirmation in a very practical way of how God does indeed speak to us if we will listen and obey."

When the team came back from the relaxing day, one of the pastors handed me a very beautiful shell nightlight, "Just a little bit of the beach," he said as he hugged me. I rejoiced with them as they related stories of the beauty of the beach and their fun in the sun. It had been a blessing day for me also and I had absolutely no regrets.

But that was not the end of the story!

Four days after coming home I was having my regular monthly retreat day with my prayer partner, Kristin. We had decided to have a picnic. So we took blankets and a sack lunch and headed down to the beach in front of the Caretakers Cabin. The sun came out and it was so quiet and peaceful we just sat silently soaking up the wonder of God's creation when suddenly a soft, gentle voice said, *"This is your day at the beach!"*

I had forgotten -

But He remembered.

My day at the beach was a *double blessing!*

A SEASON OF CHANGE

Another Call

There is a poem I love written by *J. Earnhart* the words of which could be describing the view from our window at the Shrine. I'll share just an excerpt of it so you can get a sense of why we had a longing in our hearts to live and die on the job at this idyllic place.

> "If ever seen the whales play
> Or watched the eagles in flight
> You'll remember again why you live here
> And why it feels so right...
> If ever you've seen the sunset
> As the ferry passed the shore
> You've seen the beauty of the island
> That will be with you for ever more."

We loved our job, we loved living in our log cabin, we loved the people with whom we worked and we hoped we would be there for many years to come. But on the trip to Taiwan in September, 1993, the Lord spoke to my heart in an unmistakable way. When I shared the experience with Bob we decided we needed to take time to pray and also talk with Thomas and the board as we sought to discern the next step.

We made a list of pros and con's as we prayed and walked through the weeks and months ahead while continuing to fulfill our Caretaker responsibilities. It was a two year process, but on Friday, 29th September, 1995 we shared with Thomas, "We just had a phone call from Tulsa, Oklahoma with the news that we have been unanimously accepted by the U.S.A. office for the position in China. The application papers and Tulsa staff comments have been faxed to China for their consideration. We anticipate their response sometime this week. Should we be accepted by China, it is then up to us to make the final decision. As we are going north to a prayer conference 11th - 16th October we hope to have some time there to prayerfully consider our response."

In June, 1996 Thomas wrote the following article in the Shrine of St Therese Newsletter; "With prayerful discernment and confirming signs Bob and Christie Loney applied for the Caretakers Position at the Shrine of St Therese and were accepted in the fall of 1988. Here they have served over the past several years and they each have enough unique stories of what "Caretaking" at the Shrine entails – especially the unexpected – to fill a sizable book. (Was this a prophetic statement Thomas?) In a paper prepared by *Dianne Nordling, "Missionaries out the Road"* about the Shrine and Caretaking at this place of refuge and retreat, Dianne asked the Loney's if they planned to stay indefinitely. With a grin, Christie responded, "We'll stay until they (Shrine Board) kick us out or the Lord leads us elsewhere." The Lord is leading them elsewhere, on a mission to China. We can only cooperate with that call to ministry and to pray for Bob and Christie as they respond to the Holy Spirit's direction. They have proven their faithfulness of service at the Shrine; they are ready!"

Faith or Fear

When I was nine years old my Scottish Granny gave me a plaque that hangs on the wall of our home. I have the words memorized;

"I said to the man who stood at the gate of the year, 'Give me a light that I may tread safely in to the unknown.' He replied, 'Go out into the darkness and put your hand into the hand of God that shall be to you better than a light and safer than the known way.'" M.L. Haskins.

We had been considering and praying for over two years so it had not been a spur of the moment decision, but now here we were on the threshold of a making a major change in our lives – moving to China. Not only a change of job, but we were also leaving all our family and friends behind to step into a huge abyss of 'unknown."

Faith said, "Yes" but fear had many, "What ifs"

Bob was cleaning out some files as we prepared for moving out of the cabin and sorting through what needed to be put in storage and what we could take with us, when he came across an old Denver Post newspaper. We had lived in Denver when we were first married and three of our four children were born there. The article was about an old sign that had been found above the fireplace of a 500 year old English Inn which read;

"Fear knocked at the door. Faith answered. No one was there!"

When the future is uncertain "Fear" knocks at the door in many guises and it is so easy to allow him entrance. So we began to pray and asked others to pray with us, that "Faith" would be our constant companion so *no one* would be at the door when "Fear" came knocking.

One of our last days at this absolutely, incredibly beautiful place where we had lived for eight years, a friend came to call and asked a question that had dogged my days for quite some time, "How can you leave such gorgeous scenery?" During my morning devotions just the day before, I myself had asked the Lord this very same question. His response settled it once and for all with a question of His own, "Will you worship *me* or *my creation?*" There was simply *no contest* and I had perfect peace.

In our final report as Caretakers we wrote; "It has been a busy time...we thought April was busy until we saw the May calendar which seemed to have *daily additions!* We, Bob, Thomas and I all agreed it was the busiest month since we began as Caretakers eight years previous. I don't think there were *any* days when the Lodge was not in use and many times it was back to back clean up.

We had more cooking this month than usual, The Priests, Catholic Women's group, U.S. Forest Service and the Department of Health and Social Services; also many groups wanted linens for the beds which takes more time in between groups to clean and set up again. The Post Office, Le Vasseur and Hermitage cabins had more use than usual, plus we had two Baptisms, two wedding rehearsals followed by their weddings. Every Sunday afternoon we prepared for Mass and cleaned up after the social fellowship time.

We enjoyed meeting a number of applicants for the Caretakers job, showing them around and answering questions. One inquirer, when he learned there was vacuuming, dishwashing and cooking, decided on the spot it was *not the job for him.* We have thoroughly enjoyed getting to know Chuck and Joan Gasparak, the committee's final choice for the job.

So we are moving on full of faith, knowing God's timing is always best.

A Holy Presence

June, 1996 was a hard month in terms of saying goodbye, not only to the Shrine of St Therese, but also because we sold or gave away many things we have had all our married life – thirty five years.

Bob got the lawn mowed, the first time of the season and his last on the job. Many dandelions had their beautiful yellow blossoms chopped off…sorry Thomas!

My last report for the Shrine Board included a special poem which I wrote as the result of an experience in May that same year. I had gone out to close the Chapel after a very busy day and as I walked across the causeway about 11pm there was such a peace and calm about the place. Usually I would hurry across so I could get home to bed, but as there were not many more weeks left I was just taking my time. As I opened the Chapel door and went to step inside I was overwhelmed with a sense of God's presence filling the place. So much so, that I was literally unable to enter. (It speaks in the Old Testament of the Priests not being able to go in because of the Glory of God.) I stood and waited, and after a time knew the invitation to "come on in." When I got home I wrote the following piece; except I believe it was not me, but God Himself who took pen to paper, I was just His instrument.

A Holy Presence
Awesome God you come
And meet us at the door;
In unexpected ways and
Moments unaware -
Until surrounded by yourself
We are captured in your snare.
Quite unable to move,
You hold us in that place
And fill us with your breath
Of sweetness and grace!
Around us all is quiet
No sound of angel wings
Just a steady breathing;
God fills the space.
Trembling we move
Amazed that we can
Walking in the Spirit
Enraptured in the calm -
All the days' burdens gone in a sigh
As lovingly you woo us,
"Come hither, come nigh."
Until at the altar a song begins to sing,
"Holy ground, it's holy, in the presence of the King!"

Christie Loney - 16th May, 1996

The Resurrection

THIS AND THAT

And so it is;

"Through him and for His name's sake, we received grace and apostleship to call people from among the Gentiles to the obedience that comes from faith. And you also are among those who are called to belong to Jesus Christ...Grace and peace to you from God our Father and from the Lord Jesus Christ." Romans 1:5-7 N.I.V

Each of us are called by God
To be His instruments day by day
Some at home, some far away -
Each of us have work to do
So pray for us and we'll pray for you,
Then when the trumpet sounds on that glorious day
Together
We'll hear the "Well done" He will say.
Hallelujah!

Some Favourite Recipes

One of the things we enjoyed doing, and still do, is cooking. So here are some of our favourite recipes for you to try, they may become favourites at your table also.

Mississippi Cheese Balls - Bake @ 400* for 20 minutes
1 lb sausage (I use Jimmy Dean brand)
2 cups grated cheddar cheese
2 cups Bisquick
Mix altogether. Roll into balls
Freeze leftovers and reheat as needed.

Cheese Bread Sticks – Bake @ 350* until golden brown
Cut day old bread into ½ inch thick slices. Remove crusts and spread bread with softened butter or oleo. Cut into ½ inch wide strips and roll in parmesan cheese
Allow to completely cool before storing in airtight container until ready to use.

Anne Smith's Hot Sandwiches - Place in oven @350* until heated through
Chop in food grinder:
3 cans spam or luncheon meat
1 medium onion
½ cheddar cheese
Add I can undiluted mushroom soup mix well
Fill hamburger buns. Wrap in foil (Leftovers freeze well)
Serve with carrot and celery sticks and fruit salad

Serbian Eggs – Bake @ 350* for 45 minutes or until firm to the touch
6-8 eggs well beaten. Add 1 cube melted butter (1/2 cube works for less calories)
1 cup low fat Bisquick, 1 cup non-fat milk
1 pint low fat cottage cheese (I use less)
Mix all together, pour into a 9x12 pan

Quick Apricot Salad
2 cans mandarin orange segments
1 large can pineapple tidbits, 1 can apricot or peach pie filling
2 cups mini marshmallows Mix all together and chill
Serve on lettuce as a salad or in parfait glasses as dessert

Pink Congealed Salad (Claudia Rackley)
1-3oz pkg lemon jello and 1-3oz pkg raspberry jello
1 cup boiling water 1 c Pet Milk
1 cup cottage cheese (small curd)
1 large can crushed pineapple, drained
½ cup chopped pecans or walnuts
½ cup mayonnaise
Dissolve jello and cool then add other ingredients and let set
in refrigerator.

Chocolate Zucchini Cake - Bake @ 350* for 1 hour
¾ c butter ½ c cocoa 3 eggs 1 ½ tspn soda 1 tspn cinnamon
2 tspn grated orange peel
½ c milk 2 c sugar 2 ½ c flour 2 ½ tspn baking powder
1 tspn salt 2 tspn vanilla
2 c shredded zucchini 1 c chopped nuts
Cream butter sugar and eggs until fluffy. Combine dry
ingredients in separate bowl. Add zucchini orange peel and
vanilla to creamed mixture; add dry ingredients alternately
with milk lastly add nuts.
Pour into 10" tube pan Cool 15 minutes in pan. Remove and
cool thoroughly
Frost with glaze (2 c powdered sugar 3 tblspn milk 1 tspn
vanilla)

Dump Cake - Bake @ 350 for 1 hour
Place in 9x13 pan in the following order;
1 c cherry pie filling, 1 c pineapple chunks sprinkle 1 pkg of yellow cake mix over the top. Pour on top 1 c melted oleo or butter, sprinkle 1 c grated coconut and then 1 c chopped nuts over the top. Bake and serve warm with whipped cream

Pecan Crumble Pumpkin Pie - Bake 1 hour @ 375*
1 pkg pie crust mix or home made pie crust
1 can (1 lb) pumpkin or home made
1 can (10 ozs) sweetened condensed milk
1 egg,
½ tspn ginger ½ tspn nutmeg ¾ tspn cinnamon
Pecan Topping
½ pkg pie crust mix, ½ c packed brown sugar, 1/3 c chopped nuts
Mix together until crumbly.
Combine pumpkin, milk, egg, salt, cinnamon, nutmeg, ginger and pour into pie shell. Sprinkle topping over top of filling.

Sour Cream Halibut Bake - Bake @ 500* for 10 minutes or until fish flake
1 ½ lb halibut fillets 1 cup white wine, 1 tspn salt marinate for 1-2 hours (marinate optional) Drain thoroughly on paper towels
Roll fish in 1 ½ fine toasted bread crumbs and arrange in greased baking dish
Mix together1 ½ c fine toasted bread crumbs, 1 c mayonnaise, 1 c sour cream,
¼ c finely chopped onions and spread over fish. Cover with thin layer of crumbs and dust with paprika. Serve with lemon wedges.

Tater Tot Casserole

Bake @ 375 for 30 minutes or until cheese is melted and brown on top.

Brown hamburger and chopped onion together (enough for size of group to be served) Add 1-2 cans cream mushroom soup (depends on amount of meat mixture) Place in bottom of casserole dish (9x13) or size desired

Add tater tots on top and sprinkle with grated cheddar cheese I sometimes add a layer of peas and corn on top of the meat.

End Notes and British English

For history buffs interested in more details, check out the booklet;

"Shrine of St Therese –A History of a Dream" it is a great place to begin. Also there are numerous books on St. Therese of Lisieux for whom the retreat center is named.

For more on Bishop Crimont and Father Hubbard, two books of adventure and inspiration well worth reading are,

"Dogsled Apostles" by A.H. Savage"

"Cradle of the Storms" by Bernard R. Hubbard S.J. – The Glacier Priest"

Postcards of the Resurrection Cross *in colour* are available at the Shrine of St Therese Gift Shop.

An addendum to the story, "God Bless the Cook" Oral history of early years at the Shrine has the saying, "God bless the cook" as coming from Sarah, the daughter of Caretakers Jerry and Sharon Jones. It caught on, and according to Thomas, became a regular part of their prayers when a meal was served.

British English

- For the most part spelling of words is in British English as this comes more naturally for the author.
- Dates are written: day, month, and year, this being the British norm.
- Wellingtons, sometimes referred to as "Wellies" - a British term for rubber boots
- A torch is a flashlight.
- To ring someone, means to call them on the phone. "I *rang*, but you were not home." or "Please *ring* me as soon as possible."
- Wee, simply means, small.
- A spanner is a wrench.

CPSIA information can be obtained
at www.ICGtesting.com
Printed in the USA
FFOW03n0022021217
43818580-42744FF